HUNGRY FOR GOD

O God, thou art my God,
I seek thee,
my soul thirsts for thee;
my flesh faints for thee,
as in a dry and weary land
where no water is.

(Psalm 63:1)

On the last day of the feast, the great day,
Jesus stood up and proclaimed, "If any one thirst,
let him come to me and drink. He who believes in
me, as the scripture has said, 'Out of his heart
shall flow rivers of living water.'" Now this
he said about the Spirit, which those who believed
in him were to receive; for as yet the Spirit had
not been given, because Jesus was not yet glorified.

(John 7:37–39)

HUNGRY FOR GOD

Practical Help
in Personal Prayer

RALPH MARTIN

Doubleday & Company, Inc.
Garden City, New York

Library of Congress Cataloging in Publication Data

Martin, Ralph, 1942–

Hungry for God; Practical Help in Personal Prayer.

Includes bibliographical references.

1. Pentecostalism.

2. Spiritual life—Catholic authors.

3. Prayer. I. Title.

BX2350.57.M37   248'.9'2

ISBN 0-385-09535-X Trade

0-385-09534-1 Paperbound

Library of Congress Catalog Card Number 74-4830

BOOK DESIGN BY BENTE HAMANN

ACKNOWLEDGMENTS

MEN AND WOMEN ALL OVER THE WORLD are searching for God. God can be found. Prayer is possible. I am able to live this and write this only because of the help of many, too numerous to name. But I am especially grateful to, and acknowledge the substantial contribution of, my parents, Ralph and Mary Martin; my wife, Anne, and children, John and Mary; my coworker and friend of the last ten years, Steve Clark; the nuns, priests and brothers who sacrificed their lives to make Catholic education work for me; the founders and teachers of the Cursillo Movement; my brothers and sisters, particularly the members of my household at various times, in the community I am a part of, The Word of God; and especially for the substantial editorial help of Frank Amalfitano and the more-than-secretarial help of Kathy Deering and Nancy Pflug.

CONTENTS

Part One

A Major Action of God

CHAPTER ONE

AT THE INTERSECTION
OF TRADITIONS

I T WAS A WHITE HOUSE set on the corner of a main artery feeding a residential section just off the campus of Michigan State University in East Lansing. Steve and I, both Roman Catholics, approached the door with both anticipation and nervousness. This was our first visit to an Evangelical Protestant event—a Campus Crusade for Christ meeting.

There were about eighty people in the large living room, listening to one of the Crusade's traveling staff members share his story about coming to Christ when he was in college. In the informal visiting afterwards, one of the local Crusade workers approached us and inquired if we were Christians. We had both come to a renewed personal knowledge and experience of Jesus as Lord and Savior a few years earlier, and soon convinced him that we "really knew Jesus." But when he discovered we were Catholics on the staff of the Catholic student center, working to bring students to a personal commitment to Jesus, he was flabbergasted.

The others who gathered around started describing us as "Catholic Christians" and "Catholic evangelists," terms we had never heard. I must admit, I felt as if I belonged to a supposedly extinct species and had been put on display before a marveling public. We "Catholic Christians" had stumbled into a world brand new to us, and the consternation was mutual.

In the same year, a leading Catholic magazine published a letter I had written to the president of Notre Dame University, from where I graduated in 1964. The letter spoke to the point that Notre Dame was not producing graduates with a personal commitment to the person of Christ. Crusade staff members, who by now had become warm friends, sent the letter to their national headquarters in California, and arranged for Steve and me to visit Bill Bright, president of Campus Crusade, while we were there for a summer training session.

At our meeting, we chatted amiably about the growing evangelical renewal in the Catholic Church, the return to the Bible and so on. When I innocently remarked that authentic Christianity has remained alive in every age of Catholic history, Bill bristled and soon after terminated the conversation. The period of adjustment was only beginning, and we both had a lot yet to learn: but the intersection of "Catholic Christians" and Evangelical Protestants had begun and would grow remarkably over the next few years.

That was in 1966. In the winter, friends in Pittsburgh wrote to us about the outbreak of charismatic phenomena among groups of Catholic students and faculty at Duquesne University. Steve and I tried to find out more about this by looking for some "Pentecostals" in the Lansing area. We were told of a Full Gospel Businessmen's dinner.

The speaker that night was a particularly strong-voiced evangelist from the South, trying to get people "saved and filled." We were not really struck by him, but rather by the strange kind of prayer that periodically filled the room—a singing or chanting that was different from anything we had ever heard. In the midst of this prayer, word that some

"Catholic Christians" were present reached the person leading the group. He called me to the front with an utterly
radiant smile, took out a small flask of oil and anointed my
head, praying that God would use me to preach the gospel to
Catholics. He said afterwards that he had felt "led of the
Lord" to do this. This was our first introduction to *that* kind
of language too.

A few months later, in March of 1967, while we were visiting our friends in Pittsburgh, we were prayed with for a fuller
release of God's Spirit and entered a greater freedom and
regularity in the experience of the various workings of the
Spirit.

✤

Having been born and raised a Catholic, having gone
through Catholic grade school, high school and university, I
found all this quite an experience. I was discovering worlds of
Christianity I had never known, or at least had known only
with prejudice and disdain, never with the appreciation and
sympathy that is due them. Today I remain a Catholic, not
through inertia, but by conviction, yet I have been immeasurably strengthened and formed by my contract with evangelical
Protestantism and the twentieth-century pentecostal movement.

I am not alone in this. Increasingly large numbers of
Christians of all denominations are finding themselves in the
midst of a remarkable intersection of Christian traditions, out
of which God is bringing a new and integral vision of
Christian life. In our own community here in Ann Arbor, The
Word of God, there are over 900 people from more than forty
local congregations who have come together to share their
Christian life while remaining committed to their own
churches. The result could truly be described as an evangeli-
cal-pentecostal-catholic community. There is the great stress

on personal knowledge of Jesus as Lord and Savior found in Evangelical Protestantism; the emphasis on the power of the Holy Spirit and the free expression of charismatic gifts that marks Pentecostalism; and the recognition of the tremendous importance of community unity, the place of the Eucharist and the proper role of authority within the body of Christ that is found in Catholicism.

What is happening here in Ann Arbor is happening on a worldwide level as well. An estimated 200,000 to 300,000 Catholics are now actively involved in charismatic prayer groups throughout the world. Campus Crusade is finding increasing receptivity in the Catholic Church, especially in Europe and parts of South America. Catholic priests are preaching revivals to Assembly of God pentecostal churches that need "stirring up." The Vatican initiated a five-year dialogue with classical and neo-pentecostals that has progressed remarkably smoothly.

Under the guidance of the Holy Spirit, the interaction of the various Christian traditions can produce not just an eclectic jumble which sacrifices truth to unity, but a profound integration of lost and forgotten and separated truths to produce a whole and healthy Christian life for the benefit of all the churches.

But God is not renewing and unifying Christians simply for their own sake; His purpose does not stop short with the Christian churches. God's ultimate desire and intention is that the whole world be restored to Christ, and that every man know Him directly and personally, so that once again He may exercise His lordship over the earth in a direct way. God is preparing Christians for a time of unparalleled service and mission to all men, a time of unparalleled proclamation of the Gospel—by word, by service, and by the witness of our lives together in genuine Christian community.

Dr. Albert Outler, a leading Methodist theologian, sees,

for example, the Catholic charismatic renewal as the vanguard of America's third great awakening, an event that will affect the very fabric of American life.

The baptism of the Holy Spirit as a conscious experience of conversion, the vigorous renewal of interior prayer, of small group devotions and mutual nurture, glossolalia and spiritual healing, an evangelical concern for unmediated communion with God through Christ in the Spirit—all this is happening among Catholics in many places in this country and around the world.

This isn't my bag . . . But I think I know some of the gifts and fruits of the Spirit when I see them and I am convinced that much of what I have seen is for real and just may be a portent of something very much more . . . It just might be these odd-ball Catholics with their evangelical concerns for conversion, with their charismatic baptism and tongues and with their courageous commitments to reform in both church and society who may turn out to have been the vanguards in the third great awakening this country has seen . . .
In 1960 if you said Roman Catholicism was going to start looking more evangelical than it had ever in the last 400 years, someone would have taken you off to the psychiatric ward . . . We are in the throes of an age and the birth of an age. When and how the agony will turn out, nobody knows for sure . . . in part it depends on whether Catholicism gets so embroiled in the ferment of Post Vatican II changes. Whether it gets stultified and crippled. Or whether this new outburst of freedom opens up the floodgate of charismatic, Pentecostal, spiritual renewal.[1]

Like other actions of God's Spirit, however, this renewal cannot be restricted to one nation but is quickly becoming a significant international force. Cardinal Suenens, one of the architects of Vatican Council II, sees the charismatic renewal originating in America as having a purpose in God's plan for the worldwide church.

> Something is happening in America, some new sign of hope, some star in the darkness: you are not only rediscovering Jesus as the Lord, you are also rediscovering that the Spirit of Jesus is alive today and working in your midst . . . something is here in America that will bring us to a living faith in a living God . . . I think that we have here one of the wonders of God today.[2]

If we look at the social and political circumstances surrounding this remarkable outpouring of the Holy Spirit, God's plan stands out more distinctly. The "peace and stability" of the world order rests on increasingly shaky foundations, and the ability of men to hold the social order together is more and more doubtful. But as human solutions fail and disappointments increase, people can turn from their idols more easily and turn to God Himself as the one Savior of the human race. In this situation Christians will have a remarkable opportunity to be servants of God and to shine out brightly in a world of increasing darkness.

These are truly amazing times. The tempo of God's action is increasing, and the stakes—the salvation of the race—are emerging undisguised. For the individual Christian, this is especially a time of preparation. God is preparing His people so that they can follow Him, very closely indeed. I believe that this preparation consists very centrally in becoming profoundly one with God, accustomed to hearing His voice, sensitive to the promptings of His Spirit, in full accord with His mind and heart. We must learn to obey: to go when He says go, to stop when He says stop. Only Christians who have such an abiding union with God will be able to take full part with Him in what lies ahead.

And it is through prayer that this deepening union will come to pass. Not just prayer of intercession or prayer for getting things to happen—important as that is—but prayer of friendship, prayer of joy and celebration in being with God, prayer of dedication and commitment in following Him and putting Him first in our lives, prayer of peace and silence, adoration and love.

What God is doing will affect every area of our life, as individuals and as churches. It will affect ministry and training for ministry, sacraments and their administration, mission and its methods, family life and community life, professional, economic and political life. But, it will affect none of these with the full purity and wisdom of God's love and power unless we are in very close touch with Him, increasingly possessed of His mind and heart and spirit.

What I'll be writing lays no particular claim to originality. It is, I suppose, a simple wisdom known to every age of Christians in some form or another. It is a wisdom that no man lays claim to, but a wisdom that lays claim to man. It has been immensely important to me, and will, I know, be helpful to many of us as we try to respond to what we sense God doing today. Because my roots are Catholic, this wisdom is a Catholic wisdom; but by the nature of this major action of God, it is also, and deeply, an evangelical and pentecostal wisdom.

In the course of this book I will not attempt to label what I am saying according to the tradition of Christian prayer that it derives from. I am not concerned with writing a scholarly treatise on the traditions of Christian prayer, nor am I competent to do so. I am mainly concerned to communicate what I have learned since childhood of the ways of God in prayer, and particularly what I have learned over the past ten years. My hope is not that you know more about prayer, but that you know God more, and desire Him more, and cleave to Him more.

At the outset, however, I would like to offer some outline understanding of the traditions that have influenced me, with their own peculiar strengths and weaknesses, in the hope that this may help us to be more open to and respond more fully to all that God has to offer, and understand more fully the perspective out of which I am speaking.

✳

As the Christians of the New Testament Church experienced the action of God's Spirit among them over a number of years, they tried to formulate some coherent understanding of that experience. Out of this process of reflection emerged the full understanding of the nature of the Holy Spirit and His relationship to the Father and the Son that is found in John's gospel, and later, in the creeds. As the experience of the Church grew longer, some reflection centered on the action of the Holy Spirit in the "inner man," and by the fourth century, in the writings of Clement of Alexandria, we find a fairly clear articulation of the action of the Spirit in Christian prayer.

This reflection on experience continued throughout Christian history and, in the Catholic Church at least, reached its most comprehensive and analytical attempt to understand the interior process of union with God in the writings of the Spanish mystics, John of the Cross and Theresa of Avila. While this Carmelite school of spirituality, as it is called, is by no means the only tradition of spirituality or prayer in Catholicism, it is the one that in recent centuries has most dominated the education and formation of Catholics concerned with leading a serious life of union with God.

The Carmelite tradition sees union with God in prayer occurring in a series of stages, usually identified as the purgative (emphasizing repentance for sin and initial growth in virtue), the illuminative (marked by an increased understanding and experience of God and growth in virtue) and the unitive (characterized by a profound and abiding union with God and fruitfulness of life).

The major strength of this tradition of prayer is that it focuses on God Himself—seeking Him and being fully and totally united to Him. It is also realistic: It recognizes that union with God occurs through a process of growth, requiring life-long effort and fidelity. Within the Catholic tradition, a deep understanding of the heart of man developed, and a knowledge of what must happen to that heart if man is to be fully united with God: hence, the emphasis placed on purity of heart and seeking God above all. The concrete help provided in discovering the falsity in our hearts and bringing it to the Lord is very helpful and found nowhere else in exactly the same detail and depth. It has produced a stream of life with God that runs very deep, for those who are able to progress in it, and has given a quality of depth and contemplative prayer to the Catholic Church which has been a very precious heritage.

One of its obvious weaknesses is that only a small minority of Catholics are able to seriously practice the method of prayer and make that kind of progress. The Carmelite masters speak from a different age and culture and often write in a highly technical manner geared toward a specialized group of people in specialized circumstances (the religious orders). The language is often unintelligible to the average person today and such a structured life style is not feasible for the mass of Christians.

Even within the religious orders, there are many Catholics who have worked hard for years trying to grow in prayer without seeming to make much actual contact with God. It must be said that many of these people are missing something essential to making that effort fruitful—a clear and definite personal relationship with Jesus and a release of the power of the Holy Spirit. The Catholic tradition tends to presume this initial experience, often wrongly, and concentrate on growth. People who try to grow without a solid, effective foundation in appropriating the basic realities of Christian life will have a very difficult time. Many will give up.

This is both noble and sad. Noble, because of the deep seriousness of the effort and the rightness of the goal. Sad, because it seems to reveal an impoverishment of what was normal Christian experience in the New Testament Church. The type of prayer Paul described in Romans 8:26—". . . the Spirit himself intercedes for us with sighs too deep for words" —is often pointed out as the mountain to be arrived at by strenuous effort, a mountain that only a few will finally attain.[3] In the New Testament it is presented as the normal beginning of Christian life: something that every Christian should experience through normal Christian initiation.

This is a serious weakness in the Catholic tradition—its attempt to pull itself up by its own bootstraps, insufficiently aware of the power available to the average Christian in the initial gift of the Holy Spirit. To attain the mountain of mature holiness is indeed a work of years, calling for sustained and stable growth. It is, however, a work to be assisted by a sensible experience of God and an overflowing love for Him which, if people are faithful, speeds the progress of the work. This experience puts holiness, and sustained contemplation, where it belongs—within the reach of all God's faithful, not just the especially heroic or gifted.

*

Even more than Catholic tradition, Protestant tradition is not a monolith but a number of streams and strands. Hence, it is difficult to speak conclusively of a "Protestant" tradition of prayer. However, I believe that a few helpful things could be said.

Clearly one of the greatest strengths of Protestantism has been attention to the core message of the gospel—the basic saving message of Jesus. The insights into justification by faith and obedience to the written Word of God are of fundamental importance. The Protestant tradition has correctly emphasized Jesus alone, not prayer or spirituality, as the answer to the spiritual hunger of man.

Over the past few years, we have seen a new interest develop in prayer and spirituality. People of almost every political and theological position in the churches are experiencing an actual hunger for deepened contact with God. Yet much of this, I fear, is going to miss the mark. People are being given sets of exotic techniques or "experiences," which prove to be of no lasting help, or are encouraged to persevere in a prayerful "search for God," which does nothing to relieve the agony of His absence.

In my own church, for example, there is a tendency to want to respond to the new hunger for spirituality by giving people help in prayer through group "experiences," a borrowing of techniques from Eastern religions, or help from the "tradition," which almost universally proceed on the basis of presupposing that the basic relationship with God is in good order and what is needed mainly is a spiritual tune up or return to the "sources" in prayer.

Unfortunately, in many people's lives today in the Catholic Church this is a disastrous way to proceed. Encouraging people to fill the spiritual hunger they feel by praying, giving them new techniques or "experiences" is to be leading many to a wrong perception of their situation. Often what is missing in people's lives is a clear and definite act of commitment to the person of Jesus, which gives them the basis on which to proceed with a relationship with Jesus and the Father. A person must know and experience being "reborn" in Christ (Jn. 3:5), being a "new creation" (II Cor. 5:17) in order to have the solid basis of real relationship with God in which prayer "comes naturally" and makes sense.

In addition, oftentimes what is missing is any real definite knowledge and experience of the person of the Holy Spirit. Since it is the Spirit that makes God real to us, manifests to us the Father and the Son, helps us to pray, is Christian prayer truly possible without a definite and concrete knowledge and experience of the person of Christ and the Spirit? The New Testament witness indicates not. Many people in the churches today "searching" for a fuller life with God, need to be led into an initial or renewed repentance and commitment to the person of Christ, and appropriation of the power of the Spirit, before it makes sense for them to direct their attention to growth in that relationship.

Involved as I am in a leadership role in the charismatic renewal, I come in contact with many priests and nuns, monks and contemplatives who share quite openly with me about what they've experienced in their Christian life before and since they became involved in the charismatic renewal. I'd like to have a few of them share with you in their own words what they experienced. I by no means mean to imply that people are coming to a renewed commitment to, and experience of, the person of Jesus and the power of the Holy Spirit only in the charismatic renewal—far from it; the action of

God is far wider than that—but only to illustrate how important such a fundamental renewal is to the average dedicated Catholic:

✠

An Older Nun:

For over sixty years of my religious life, I could not meditate. I tried every method; the sisters tried to teach me, but all in vain. The best I could do was to read little prayers and try to keep my mind on what I read. After receiving the baptism of the Holy Spirit, I am living a new life. Christ has become real. He is alive. I feel His presence in me, around me. When I read Holy Scripture it means something to me. Now I can see meaning in the Bible stories; they apply to me; they are real. Christ talks to me; I talk to Him. Meditation is a real spiritual joy. Time goes so fast; an hour slips by before I'm finished talking with Him. Even my love for people is different. The peace and joy I now experience cannot be described. After all these years, at the age of eighty-four, I am beginning a new life. I have a new awareness of Christ's presence in my life. Praise the Lord. Sr. Melita[4]

✠

A Rector of a Seminary:

I felt personally inadequate before a job for the first time in my life. Many times I had tried to be number one, doing everything by myself, only to have things end in ruin. When I was studying at Harvard, I tried so hard to be the best student that they finally had to carry me off to the infirmary for some rest. Later I became a Judge Advocate in the Air Force and immediately tried to solve all the military justice problems in the Eastern United States. Again I collasped from exhaustion. I did the same thing in some of my inner city work, letting the problems and work load build up to the point of collapse. This

*time I knew I couldn't wait until the work ended in dis-
aster before turning to the Lord for help. I told the Lord
that this was the end, and did my best to ask Him to take
over.*

*I hadn't read anything about Catholic pentecostals ex-
cept some sensational headlines and stories about kooky
things going on at Notre Dame, and I was not inclined to
pursue it. Yet when a very close friend of mine, the su-
perior of a women's Carmelite monastery nearby, told me
about being baptized in the Holy Spirit, I don't remember even questioning what she said. We sat in the visiting
room of the seminary and she just told me very simply
what had happened to her since being prayed with. I
thought to myself: "Yes, yes, this has to be for me. If
being baptized in the Spirit can make such fantastic
changes in her after years of living the contemplative
life, then it's definitely something I need right now."*

*I had to wait about five weeks. I read a little, but
mostly just got more and more hungry for the Spirit
. . . Then, Fr. Jim Ferry from New Jersey came to the
seminary with a group of young people to give a talk.
His talk was about Christ, and every time he mentioned
the name "Jesus" it was like someone setting off sparks
in me. The desire for Jesus was so strong I felt it would
break through my chest. Later, Fr. Jim asked if anyone
wanted to pray for anything. Before I knew it, I was
kneeling in the middle of a group of about thirty people
asking to be baptized in the Holy Spirit. They laid hands
on me, and immediately I received a tremendous sense of
being, deep within me. It was glorious. I later joined a
group praying over a priest for an increase in wisdom.
But every time I tried to pray over this man in English,
it came out in another tongue. That night, I woke up
about twelve times to find myself praying. It was prayer*

*I had never known before, a beautiful sense of the Holy
Spirit crying out inside me.*

*My life and work as a priest changed totally and dra-
matically, my preaching became a proclamation of the
Good News of Christ. My counseling started to include
more prayer for healing. My confessional work started to
involve revelatory gifts such as knowing what a person's
problem was before he said it, to seeing a completely
different approach to a problem than the one the person
had. Prayer itself eventually took on a more contemplative orientation, I violated the rules I set for myself as a
busy college administrator and gave the time between
eight and ten every morning to the Lord, and found that
I accomplished more between ten and twelve than I use
to between eight and twelve.*

*One of the biggest changes I experienced was a new
courage and strength to state what I knew was right,
even though my statements might be uncomfortable and
unpopular. This happened most dramatically in connection with the conspiracy trial of Fr. Philip Berrigan and
the others in Harrisburg . . .*[5]

*

A Catholic Bishop:

*For me a bishop is someone who has to unite a local
church. As I began to experience the pluralism, indeed
division, in the church today, I started looking for an answer, some way to make the church one. I noticed how
St. Paul handled the problem of polarization between
the Hellenists and the Jews in the early church. He didn't
approach it directly but rather drew their attention to the
person of Jesus, insisting that in Jesus we find the key to
the answers we are seeking to all our problems. I knew
that what I was looking for as a key to the unity of the
church had to do somehow with centering our lives on
Christ.*

I went to a theological institute on Jesus Christ and listened to theologians. I came back feeling sad because I didn't find the answer, only questions. But then in the experience of a prayer retreat, led by a priest who was deeply involved in the charismatic renewal—Fr. George Kosicki—I found the key. It is centered in the realization that Jesus Christ is Lord. Our whole theology can be plugged into that statement, and it pulled things together for me . . . I think we're taking the heart of Christianity—the person of Jesus—for granted. When we're attracted to that person, in personal union with Him, then He will teach us the truths that keep us in unity. . . . Sometimes even in statements that we bishops put out we're a little heavy on "the Church teaches." Sometimes we don't quite make clear the centrality of commitment to the person of Jesus that is needed to make the teachings make sense and to motivate people. . . . At the end of that retreat I asked to be prayed over for a deeper work of God's Spirit in me. That began my contact with the charismatic renewal, and the deepening of my own prayer life and experience of the working of the Spirit.

This power of the Holy Spirit that has been released in my life through the charismatic renewal became particularly clear to me when I had to give a retreat for priests. As you know, giving a retreat for priests these days is quite a challenge. I think I spent two months preparing for it and had eighteen talks ready. But then I felt I should go away for a day just to pray and fast to prepare for it. During that day the Spirit began to show me that, in addition to preparing talks, I had to be open too and to expect His help and guidance on the spot. The Spirit said that I had to be open to Him helping me understand where the men were and what their real needs were. And the experience of that retreat was tremendous for me because I found priests listening.

At the end of the retreat an older priest came up quietly just to say, "Bishop, I'm deeply grateful for this retreat. I don't recall in fifty years ever having attended one that had this kind of power with me. We really needed this." My reaction was one of "Isn't this wonderful! Praise the Lord!" but at the same time, I wondered if the young priests had been reached. Then three young priests came to me after the retreat to say they felt they were beginning to find their way out of confusion. They attributed this feeling primarily to the insistence during the retreat that we must center our lives on Jesus Christ as our Lord, and be men of prayer.

I had a similar experience giving a retreat at a seminary where the seminarians were terribly divided and the community fragmented. On the retreat I preached the basic gospel message, of the living person of Jesus as Lord. Afterwards the rector said that the results of the retreat could be summed up in the remarks of one student who put it like this: "Before the retreat I didn't think that even Jesus Christ could unite this community, but somehow He did it through the bishop."

These are results of a power working through us that we can't claim originates with us; it is the power of the Holy Spirit Himself, and it produces results far beyond what merely human effort alone produces. It is this working of the Spirit through me, in preaching, in counseling, in prayer, that I've begun to experience in a new way through the charismatic renewal.[6]

Prayer is *not* God's primary way of coming to us. We are saved by faith in Jesus, and not by our efforts at prayer or at anything else, including morality. Many of us are in need not of new techniques or a new understanding of prayer, but of a reconsideration of where we stand as regards Jesus of Nazareth, and what our personal response to Him is. He is not the dogmatic background or popular symbol of Christianity, but the living person at the heart of it. He desires to be the living person at the heart of our life and at the heart of our prayer life. He desires to release the power of the Spirit into our lives. The genius of Protestant spirituality is this very emphasis. It is an emphasis that can easily get lost and has certainly done so in large parts of Catholicism today.

At the same time, because of Protestant reaction to Catholic sacramentalism, some of the developments of the religious life, and the "perfection of the few" strains in Catholicism, this tradition has also been marked by a suspicion of the contemplative life, especially devoted to union with God in prayer, simply for the sake of God Himself.

Personal prayer, and having set times to pray, have sometimes been classed by Protestants as "Catholic" things. Dr. Hallesby, a famous Scandinavian church leader and writer earlier in this century, quotes some responses he received when suggesting a personal prayer time to people:

> Why should we have definite seasons of prayer? Is not this a hangover of salvation by good works? Isn't there something Catholic about it?[7]
> The Lord certainly does not expect people who are well and strong . . . able to work, to pray so much . . . isn't this a Catholic idea?[8]

Dr. Tozer, writing somewhat later from America, makes a moving summons to evangelical Christians to seek a deeper relationship with the Lord Himself, to know Him more and be with Him in prayer.

> In our day everything is made to center upon the initial act of "accepting" Christ (a term, incidentally, which is

not found in the Bible) and we are not expected there-
after to crave any further revelation of God to our souls.
We have been snared in the coils of a spurious logic
which insists that if we have found Him we need no
more seek Him. This is set before us as the last word in
orthodoxy, and it is taken for granted that no Bible-
taught Christian ever believed otherwise . . . In the
midst of this great chill there are some I rejoice to acknowledge, who will not be content with shallow logic.
They will admit the force of the argument, and then turn
away with tears to hunt some lonely place and pray, "O,
God, show me thy glory." They want to taste, to touch
with their hearts, to see with their inner eyes the wonder
that is God.[9]

In popular Protestant books such as *The Kneeling Christian*,
there is a tendency to look upon union with God as a means
rather than an end; effective intercessory prayer is often the
focus of Protestant treatises on prayer. And quite recently a
Methodist campus minister, writing on the state of Christian
life on campus commented on "the affective aridity of most
Protestant worship."[10]

*

As early as 1958, Henry Van Dusen, then president of
Union Theological Seminary, identified the pentecostal movement that had sprung up in America at the turn of the
twentieth century as a third force in Christianity, with a
significance comparable to the then existing, two forces of
Protestantism and Catholicism.[11] His remarks have proven
remarkably accurate. The worldwide charismatic renewal has
as yet only begun to have its full impact on the Catholic and
Protestant churches, but it has already profoundly affected
them. With a seventy-year history, we cannot speak very
helpfully about traditions of prayer: The significance of the

charismatic renewal is not in its traditions, which do exist, but in the fact that it is, in essence, a vital manifestation of the Spirit of God Himself, with a force and scope that has not been seen since New Testament times.

It brings no new revelation, but a vivid actualization of what both Protestant and Catholic traditions hold as important. It is common for Catholics and Protestants involved in the charismatic renewal to say that their traditions have come to life for the first time. Its contribution is to allow us to experience our traditions with something of their original power and impact.

At the same time, as a third party, it is enabling Catholics and Protestants to sort out their traditions and accept things from one another that would at one time have been unthinkable. The Spirit at work in this renewal is bringing a searching light to bear on our traditions and lives, and He is enabling us to move forward, faithful to what is best in our traditions but not defensively or neurotically or fearfully locked to them.

Charles Simpson, a Baptist minister, seems to say it best.

One of the contrasts we've noticed in our contacts with Catholics in the charismatic renewal is an emphasis lacking in most Protestant circles. Catholics generally emphasize the whole process of salvation, whereas Protestants, at least my kind, tend to emphasize the initial new birth. The two truths, which have been kept isolated so long, need to be taken together. If we see all of Christianity as being wrapped up in the new birth, we miss (I'll use a word we don't use often) the sacramental aspects of the fellowship of the Church. If we don't get the starting point, we might think we can grow in the Church without ever getting plugged in spiritually. Both truths are needed for the Church to be what it needs to be. The Catholic tradition tends to produce a few spiritual giants, the evangelical tradition produces a lot of spiritual babies. We need babies, a lot of them, if the Church is to grow, but those babies need to grow up and reproduce themselves if the Church is going to be real. We have to take the two truths together.[12]

Being open to what God is teaching us through one another, about ourselves and our traditions, and through the third force God is using, the charismatic renewal, seems to be an imperative for one concerned about union with God in prayer today. As personal a thing as prayer is being profoundly affected by the larger thing God is doing in the ecumenical renewal of His Churches. My attempt in this book is to bring these two truths or traditions together, as their unity is being lived in my life and the life of growing numbers of Catholics and Protestants around the world.

Part Two

Knowing God

CHAPTER TWO

THE ENCOUNTER
WITH JESUS

An aborigine in the outback of modern Australia looks at the sun and sky, and dreams.

A government official in France is present at the birth of his first child, feels stirred by an emotion of gratitude to a God he does not believe in, and is confused.

A nominally Christian military officer in a progressive African state, terrified of the power of evil spirits that the Christian missionaries assure him do not exist, sends out word that he needs a sacrifice to protect him from their power: the son of the local grain merchant is found dead the next day from unexplained causes.

A man in a drugstore in Chicago stands before a revolving rack of paperback books and finally chooses one that promises it will enable him to harness supernatural forces to better his life.

On a hilltop on a little-visited Pacific island, a group of men and women huddle around the likeness of an airplane, fervently hoping and praying that the god who brings material blessings in airplanes will return and make their life a better one.

Who is God? How often has that question been asked?

How many men and women have looked up in fear at the

thunder or the shadows of the forest and wondered about the power they sensed beyond the natural processes of the world and life? How many men and women in sophisticated drawing rooms have wittily discussed the existence and nature of God? How many books have been written, cries of rage and frustration been uttered, tears of despair been shed? Whether inarticulately, with sighs and groans too deep for words, or in a polished, civilized discourse, man has agonized over the question of God.

Who is God? Nearly four thousand years ago a semi-nomad in the Middle East heard the voice of God tell him to take all he had and move to a new land. His name became Abraham. To this man, and to his descendants, the God whom men search for began to reveal Himself in what was to be a definitive way.

To this tiny people He revealed Himself as one, as the supreme power of the universe, pre-eminent over all others. He promised them that, if they were faithful to Him, they would prosper beyond any other people and experience a goodness of life beyond their own power.

He promised to reveal Himself and His purpose and the purpose of the world. He made it clear that He was choosing to begin this revelation with them, not because of their merits but simply because He chose them.

They responded, enough at least for Him to make them into a definite people, whose existence was explicitly founded on their adherence to Him, the people of Israel. They experienced, when they were faithful, prosperity and protection from their enemies. When they were unfaithful, He let them experience the consequences of life apart from Him. They were plundered by other nations, experienced bad government and civil disorder, and were eventually driven from their land.

As this people grew in relationship with their God, they came to understand that His creation had been mortally damaged with the co-operation of the human race, whom He had created to live as His sons. This rebellion had caused the fear and mistrust and hate and jealousy and lust that now dominated human life and had their physical effects in sickness, disease and eventually death, and their social effects in poverty, war, racism and loneliness.

God began to make it clear that He wanted to restore the human race to its original purpose—an uninterrupted life of union with Him and one another in harmony with the whole creation. He began to speak to Israel through His prophets, telling them of a time that was coming when men would be fully restored to union with Himself, when knowledge of Himself would cover the earth as do the waters of the sea.

He spoke to them of a time when men would be given a new heart. He told them of a harmony that He was intending to restore throughout the universe, when the lion would lie down with the lamb, when nations would beat their swords into plowshares and when He would resume the direct governance of the human race.

In the midst of these prophecies, one strand told of the person through whom God would accomplish this restoration: His servant, the Messiah. Yet few were prepared for Jesus of Nazareth.

There were those in Israel who expected God's salvation to be immediately effective in the political and military realm, freeing Israel, by force of arms, from the occupation forces of the Romans. When they saw that Jesus was not moving to such an immediate goal as this, they abandoned Him.

There were others in Israel who had hardened in their role as "defenders of the faith" and had become concerned only with adherence to custom and the letter of the law. Jesus re-

buked them for the self-will at the heart of their stance, and
they encouraged the Romans to execute Him.

Jesus did not fit any of the political or theological cate-
gories of the time. He had not come to support a party or
position, but to bring about a full restoration of the human
race. He had come to offer men an intimacy with God and
one another that few could even comprehend. He broke
through established patterns of religious thinking and con-
founded the religiously learned.

The Greeks, too, who had produced a body of religious
philosophy that some early Christians considered a second
Old Testament, had difficulty accepting the person of Jesus.
Used to a variety of religious expressions and theories, they
could find the story of Jesus interesting, but they backed
away from accepting Him on His own terms. They could accept gods and theories of gods, but not the incarnation and
resurrection of the only Son of God.

If God was revealing Himself more definitively in the person of Jesus, why was it such a difficulty for the Jews, who
had already known Him in a real way, and for the Greeks,
who prided themselves on a searching spirit? What was God
doing in Jesus that made Paul speak of Him as "a stumbling
block to Jews and folly to Gentiles" (I Cor. 1:23)?

At the heart of this, and I believe, all resistance to accepting Jesus as He presents Himself to us in Scripture and in the
other ways in which we encounter Him (in prayer, accidental
"moments," in preaching, in testimony, in the depths of our
heart, in stirrings of our conscience, our memory) is one
manifestation or another of the fundamental sickness affect-
ing our race, conscious or unconscious rebellion against the
full reign of God over His creation, sin. The initial aim of
Jesus was to preach repentance from sin and its forgiveness;
at heart this was a proclamation for men to shift the basis
of their life from self-centered to God-centered, from being

their own men to being God's men. It was a proclamation
that implied a yielding up of all a man's resources, beliefs,
attitudes, plans, and a willingness to have God order them for
His glory and for our good. It meant giving up one's autonomy and independence, and living life under the rule of God
and His Spirit. It was a call to men to make a new start, a
new beginning, to be "born again." It was a call to get into
the right relationship with God, to have one's heart and life
right with God. When a man meets the Word and person of
Jesus any pockets or stratas of rebellion, independence, anything that isn't submitted to God and His rule is challenged,
feels uncomfortable, and in that encounter, that moment of
challenge, either responds in surrender or resists.

Resistance and surrender are at the heart of the Christian
life; I have known and do know both. Perhaps some of my
own experiences can help demonstrate what goes on in a
man's heart as Jesus attempts to reveal Himself to him.

I was born and grew up in what would be called a good
Catholic family. As a child I had a deep and personal relationship with the Lord. I loved Him, wanted to be close to
Him, knew He loved me, and never wanted to offend Him. I
took Him and Christianity seriously.

As I went through high school, however, I questioned my
religion. I was dissatisfied with the answers I received and
began to doubt the truth of Christianity. I developed a harsh,
critical spirit that looked at the Lord and the Church at a
distance from the world of my own mind and heart.

At Notre Dame, my criticism continued. I became convinced that truth and vitality were not to be found in the
"official" Church. I looked more and more to philosophy,
literature, and "life experiences" to find something of life and
truth.

I was particularly impressed with the harsh questioning
and intense honesty of the German philosopher Nietszche.

He had foreseen from the nineteenth century the present "God is dead" movement. The roots of faith in Western culture had been cut long before. God's existence had become more and more an academic question, irrelevant to life as it was actually lived. I too could see no appreciable quality in the lives of my Christian acquaintances that could be traced to their Christianity. I could say with Nietszche, "Christians would have to look more redeemed for me to believe in their Redeemer."

During this time, different people tried to respond to my questioning with advice. One person suggested that I get involved with the "new liturgy" to find the meaning of Christianity. I attended one liturgy with music by Bob Dylan and Simon and Garfunkel, where people hugged one another. I thought that if someone wanted to listen to music and hug people, he did not need to dress it up in religious language to make it acceptable. Another person suggested I get involved in Christian social action, and see the meaning of Christianity in serving others. I attended a few meetings of a Christian group discussing world poverty, and left feeling that there were more effective secular agencies to deal with the problems: it was not necessary to be a Christian to care about others. What people were suggesting as unique and important about Christianity seemed at most to be only leftover cultural associations from a time when Christianity did mean something.

In order to afford school during my senior year, I had to accept a graduate student's offer to share the custodian's quarters in the campus art gallery. The only drawback was that Phil was a committed Christian.

Halfway through that year, he attended something called a *cursillo* (pronounced coor-see-yo—Spanish for "little course"), a type of retreat that was developing into a renewal movement in the Catholic Church. (Over a million Catholics have made one world wide, and in many ways this movement prepared the way for the charismatic renewal in the Catholic Church, while continuing to exercise a unique contribution of its own.) He came back from it decidedly different. There was a new joy in his life, and a new experience of the presence of God.

Eventually, he got me to sign up for a cursillo too. The people in charge decided to accept my application, although they considered me a poor risk. A few days before it was to begin, however, I decided I could not possibly go—graduation was only a few months away and I had a great deal of work to do.

I sensed something happening in Phil then that moved me. I sensed him loving me, and knowing that another person loves you can do something to even the hardest of hearts. I finally gave in. But first I warned Phil that I wouldn't prostitute my intellectual honesty by pretending to experience something while other, simpler, people mistook emotional excitement for a religious experience. I was a "liberated" man, freed by the incisive Nietszchean intellect from the pious beliefs of my childhood. With all that understood, I went away for the weekend retreat.

During the first day of the cursillo I admired the group dynamics of the weekend and could see how some people would be taken into thinking that they were going to have a religious experience. I admired the mind of the person who developed the cursillo. I then began to admire the mind of the person who invented Christianity, as I found the imagery and themes of Christianity fascinating. I began to get an uneasy feeling that I was perceiving something of the mind of God Himself.

In the talks, a variety of people—insurance men, state legislators, teachers—spoke of Jesus as of a person they knew and were in relationship with. I felt uncomfortable and

THE ENCOUNTER WITH JESUS

wished they would speak of Christ or the Second-Person of the Trinity or something with a bit more theoretical distance. Either they were into a relationship with Jesus Himself or they were crazy.

I began to sense His presence, as if He were in the room. A struggle went on; if I admitted He existed, was the Son of God, and had risen from the dead, there would be no recourse but to be His disciple—there was nothing more important in the world than the reality of God and His call to us.

Memories of past experiences ran through my mind—being overwhelmed by a starry night, being on the point of bursting at the beauty of a day, the love of good friends, childhood joys. I sensed that He was present in all of them, with me all the time.

I wanted to come to Him now, but a nagging obstacle remained. They talked of sin and of the need to repent and to ask forgiveness. This was a problem. I had stopped believing in sin, and what people called sin I had come to calling "learning experiences": "things that normally occurred in the course of growth, things that were part of life, no matter the pain or hurt, but nothing to be forgiven for." I prided myself on being honest and a searcher for truth and had pretty much suppressed any awareness of being responsible in any way for anything wrong I had done. Then I began to get a dim sense, which grew into fully painful sight, that there was some fundamental ways in which I was blind to the condition of my own heart.

Somewhere along the years something had insinuated itself into what had perhaps begun as an honest questioning and search for truth, that tended to resist and even block out the truth. I desired to see and believe only as it suited me. I had made myself the creator of my own universe, the lord of my own and others' lives, the arbiter of my own morality.

There was something in me, I was forced to tragically admit, that didn't want to know the truth at all, that wasn't honestly searching at all, but was carefully choosing to perceive only those things that would allow me to persist as king of my universe. To find the truth would involve acknowledging the existence and nature of one who would shed a horribly tearing light on my own life. I realized that every time I had come close to finding the truth of God I had decided to try another path; every time I had begun to hear His voice calling me, I had drowned it in noise or laughter or music or violence. Every time I had caught a glimpse of Him in a situation out of the corner of my eye, I had turned away to reassure myself with the reality of material creation—using the creation to escape the Creator!

By God's grace, at the end of that cursillo, I was given enough courage to admit the truth of my condition, the reality of the Lordship of Jesus, to kneel down and confess my sin, renounce it, and turn over my life to Him. I experienced the release of God's power within me and came to know Him in an incredibly full way—with a bursting heart and tears of love and joy. Three years later I was to understand that I had experienced what people call being baptized in the Spirit.

It's been over ten years since that last weekend in February of 1964 when I was able to acknowledge Jesus in all His magnificence and holiness and purity and presence, confess my fundamental and specific sin to Him, and ask Him to take over my life. It was a new beginning, but just a beginning. It wasn't that I wasn't a Christian before that. I was for many years. But it was beginning again; and it has continued. The details of the last ten years aren't relevant at the moment. Suffice it to say that by God's grace I persevered in the simple means of growth, daily prayer, Christian community, He had shown me at the beginning and in the fundamental acknowledgment of Him as my Savior and

Lord, renewed numerous times. It has allowed Him to deepen His hold upon me and purify me, although not without suffering and pain, and not without subsequent discoveries, that I expect will continue to happen, of further levels of my being that need to be more deeply yielded to Him. What I want to draw our attention to now is how important our fundamental attitudes toward Him are; how important it is to open our heart to His light, and if there be anything not right there in our fundamental relationship with Him, ask Him to help us get it right.

I haven't shared personally in order to propose my experience as a "model" for others to imitate in seeking God's action in their own lives. It isn't and shouldn't be considered as such. The circumstances of each of our lives are different and it is a mistake to try to make another's circumstances our own. What I have shared I have done so in an attempt to lay bare in a detailed and experiential manner some of the fundamental dynamics of the resistance of our hearts to the Lordship of Christ, in the hope that it may be useful in helping us examine our own hearts for any traces of rebellion or resistance and be encouraged to let go of them to receive Him more fully, in our lives; in our circumstances.

For some this process of conversion to Jesus and of receiving the Spirit is sudden and dramatic, as it was in my case. For others it is gradual, taking place, sometimes in what seems to be imperceptible stages, over a period of time, even years. But it is the same Lord, doing the same work in what fundamentally are the same fearful, resistant hearts.

Whether we are not yet Christians or whether we have been Christians for a long time, much of what happens in prayer is a result of what has happened on the level of our fundamental decisions and attitudes in relation to Jesus. The more specific we see the revelation of God in Christ to be, the more specific becomes the possibility of our response.

The more total we see the self-giving of God in Christ to be, the more total becomes the possibility of our response to Him.

There are those of us, and perhaps all of us at times, who would prefer that the mystery that had been hidden for the ages had remained hidden and had not been revealed as starkly and as concretely as it was in Jesus. There are those of us who find God distant and, whatever we might say on a conscious level, prefer that He remain distant. There are those of us who find God vague and diffuse and in hidden ways want Him to remain that way. When God is vague and distant our following of Him can be vague and distant and leave us with the experience of a "good conscience." When God is close and specific and concrete, it calls for a response to Him that both allows and demands a more total yielding of our lives in specific ways. A personal God can claim a personal response of me in my most unique and innermost depths. There must be an inevitable moment of crisis when the claims of Jesus become irreconcilable with my style of life.

Unfortunately, in wide sectors of the Church today, we have accepted a view that assumes the good will of everything and everyone, including ourselves. The sober yet life-giving realism of the Judeo-Christian tradition invites us to perceive the condition of the human heart, and see how desperately corrupt its deeper runnings can be and are. To go on with Jesus to God in prayer involves more than learning techniques or perseverance; it raises and invites a fundamental consideration or reconsideration of how totally we have accepted Him, given ourselves to Him, embraced Him and accepted His claims.

Jesus cannot conveniently be accepted as a "great teacher" and added to a list of great men to be invoked to support our world view or cause. C. S. Lewis notes:

A man who was merely a man and said the sort of things Jesus said would not be a great moral teacher. He would either be a lunatic—on a level with the man who says he is a poached egg—or else he would be the Devil of Hell. You must make your choice. Either this man was, and is, the Son of God: or else a madman or something worse. You can shut Him up for a fool, you can spit at Him and kill Him as a demon; or you can fall at His feet and call Him Lord and God. But let us not come with any patronising nonsense about His being a great human teacher. He has not left that open to us. He did not intend to.[1]

He was neither a lunatic nor a fiend. However strange or terrifying or unlikely it may seem, I must accept that He was and is God. If that is true, the proper response is to fall on my knees in adoration and surrender. If He were merely a great teacher or "ideal" or "founder," He could be consulted, or admired, or quoted, but not adored.

The emptiness that haunts the vision of Buddha, the darkness that lies over the world of Allah, the frustration of suffering, death and injustice that plagues the Jews are shattered in the resurrection of the Son of God from the dead. The human race is restored to its destiny, eternal life, when Jesus breaks the chain that ties all creation to death and decay. He sets us free of the bonds that hold us in misery and fills us, not just with an absence of pain or an annihilation of personal consciousness, but a fullness of personal life. Into the silence of the East, a Word is spoken; into the darkness of the West, a light shines. The Word is a person, the light has a name: Jesus, Son of God, Savior, Door to the Father.

CHAPTER THREE

SHOW US THE FATHER

THE DAY was quickly waning and the street lights had just come on. I pulled the collar of my jacket up and leaned against a telephone pole, waiting for a bus back across the river to the city in the distance. I had just come from visiting a friend in Union City, New Jersey, and was beginning the first leg of the return trip, through New York City, to Princeton, New Jersey, where I was studying philosophy in my first year of graduate school. As I stood there I felt some of the loneliness that all of us feel at times, especially when we've left someone we're close to, and are, once again, alone.

That loneliness was sharpened into something like pain as I watched the lights of houses come on and the dusk thicken and settle, and experienced on a level deeper than most of us can articulate, the background sorrow that haunts our race, as day turns into night, and one season to another, with a relentlessness and implacability that leaves its marks of age on us, separates us from our friends, and finally from life itself, as the last night of all comes, the night of death. Who can articulate what we feel as we experience the great cosmic realities of space and time, apart from our control, moving us toward our death, separating us from our fellow men, tearing momentary happiness and stability, touches of eternity, from our hand and lengthening the loneliness of separation and loss in the ultimate separation and loneliness of death itself. As each year goes by and we see the leaves darken and fall, the snows and frost come to the barrenness of winter trees, our friends sicken and die, suffer financial loss, have their children leave home, have yet another war break out, see the marks of aging in our own bodies, we increasingly wonder and yet are afraid of the answer to the question, "can life itself be saved?"

We find, no matter how firmly we attempt to grasp and hold it, that life, with its relationships and possessions and hopes and dreams and desires, slips through our fingers. We are powerless to possess it, powerless to stop the relentless movement toward the end, death.

How we would have liked to love that person better; how we regret what we did in that situation; how we would have liked to hold on to that beautiful day, that moment of love, that hope of happiness. We are powerless to stop it. We can delay it, we can erect walls to slow it down or drown it out—money, medicine, music, work, relationships, theories, projects—but it relentlessly pushes through and we are all overcome, destroyed.

It all ends.

Our face smarts from the discipline. We are stunned by the deafness that meets our agonizing pleas for mercy. We are made desperate in our inner being as day passes into night. For us, each day the separation from life itself progresses.

Who can save us from the relentless course of this life, which mercilessly proceeds to death?

But when the time had fully come, God sent forth his Son, born of woman, born under the law, to redeem those who were under the law, so that we might receive adoption as sons. (Gal. 4:4–5)

Even as I felt pain and loneliness on that street corner in Union City, I experienced in a new and greatly intensified way what I had already begun to experience during the eight months of my revitalized commitment to Jesus—that God was *my Father*. It was as if God was taking off the wraps and letting me "see" more deeply and vividly how deep His love is, and how personal His relationship is to me as my Father. I began to say over and over again, "Father, Father, Father," slowly, sometimes softly under my breath, sometimes silently.

By bearing the affliction and misery of the human situation, even suffering death at our hands, Jesus has opened a way to save life from the process of death. When death had spent its full force, His Father raised Him from the dead, revealing His glory and power as the only Son of God. Passing over from death to the glory of life forever, He promised that if those who heard His Word and hungered for salvation put their faith in Him, they would experience a new relationship with God. They would become, with Jesus, His beloved sons, have life now in a totally new way, and share eventually in the actual physical resurrection of the body.

When we sense the presence of God in Jesus and open our hearts to Him, His Spirit becomes joined to our spirit. In a mysterious but very real and experiential way, we begin to partake of a new life that is not subject to sin and death. We walk in newness of life that consists not simply in the forgiveness of sin, but also in the discovery that the Father of Jesus is now our Father.

There are "seasons" of God's action in our life—times when He's stirring things up, and times when things seem to be quiet. At these special moments and turning points, some more decisive than others, the Spirit leads us into a deeper experience of God, not for the sake of experiences, but for the sake of a deeper and more abiding union with Him. The Spirit unites with our weak and ignorant spirits, and helps us to know, in a way that affects our emotions and memories, our past experiences and present fears, the all-surpassing love God the Father has for us.

Standing in the cold at the bus stop saying over and over again, "Father, Father, Father," was such a turning point in my awareness of who He is to me. There have been others, and each one has drawn me into a deeper freedom from anxiety and a greater confidence in what God has for me.

When my first child was born four years ago, I went to look at him in the nursery. As I looked at him, something opened up deep within me. I had never experienced the love a father has before. It was partly my instinct as a man for his first-born child, but it was also the Father within me working through me to be a father to my son, John. I experienced a depth and tenderness of love of John that I had never experienced before. Through it I learned of the depth and even the fierceness of the love of God for us, His children.

Sometimes we hear that a person without a good earthly father can never hope to understand what it means that God is our Father. Sometimes we are told that people cannot know the love of God the Father and know Christ as their Savior unless their standard of living is first raised through economic and political liberation. Such myths come out of ignorance of the burning love of God and His awesome power in drawing men to Himself in the midst of every circumstance. I have seen many people who suffered abuse and neglect from their human fathers directly experience the love of God and learn from that what a Father is. I know of people in the slums of

South American cities whose hearts are bursting with the love of God the Father poured into them by the Spirit. God can overcome any obstacle to show men His love and draw them into sonship.

Encountering God in the person of Jesus and coming to grips with His claims as Savior and Lord is a significant, decisive, step in coming to know God. Jesus is *the* door of direct and personal access to God, but our commitment to Jesus only opens the door. We are intended by God to walk through it into the fullness of His life. Those who have committed their lives to Jesus can expect Him to unfold to them a deeper and deeper knowledge and experience of God.

At the heart of Jesus' desire for His disciples is that they come to know God as their Father. In the last days of His earthly life, in fact, He spoke urgently and clearly of the relationship His disciples were to have to God as their Father, similar to the relationship that Jesus Himself had with the Father.

As we commit our lives to Jesus, and accept Him as our Savior and Lord, we need to let Him show us the Father.

The disciples had a difficult time understanding much of what Jesus was about. Jesus spoke frequently throughout His life about the Father, and yet a few days before He died, Philip, out of the frustration of not quite understanding, asked Him, "Lord, show us the Father, and we shall be satisfied" (Jn. 14:8). Jesus' response was striking. "Have I been with you so long, and yet you do not know me, Philip? He who has seen me has seen the Father . . . The words that I speak to you I do not speak on my own authority; but the Father who dwells in me does his works. Believe me that I am in the Father and the Father in me; or else believe me for the sake of the works themselves" (Jn. 14:9–11).

When we first think of in what way Jesus reveals who God

is to us, we think of His mercy and compassion in forgiving sin and healing the sick and conclude from these, rightly, that Jesus reveals to us the mercy and compassion of God. But Jesus is intent not just on revealing the characteristics or attributes of God, but the identity of the persons of God, the astounding fact that God is a union of three persons and that it is into that union that He invites His disciples.

With this in mind, read the gospel of John and notice the remarkable frequency with which Jesus speaks of His Father, and the remarkable things He indicates about the relationship They are in. Seeing what relationship the Father and Son are in is very important, for it is precisely this relationship that we are offered a part in; it is into this relationship that Jesus has been preparing us to be drawn.

As I read John's gospel I counted 108 references that Jesus makes to His Father. He always talks about His Father and the picture that emerges of the relationship is one in which there is an utterly profound commitment of love between the Father and the Son, and a total self-giving of one to the other.

Jesus time and time again clearly indicates that He is fully obedient to the Father (Jn. 8:28–29), does nothing on His own authority and only does what pleases the Father, and that He is set on not doing His own will, but "the will of the one who sent me" (Jn. 6:38). Jesus indicates again and again that He teaches and speaks only what the Father gives to Him to teach and speak (Jn. 8:26–29) and indeed, that "the Son can do nothing of his own accord, but only what he sees the Father doing; for whatever he does, that the Son does likewise" (Jn. 5:18–19, 30). Jesus even states that what He lives or subsists on, what is food to Him, is "to do the will of the one who sent me, and to complete his work" (Jn. 4:34).

Just as Jesus does everything to please the Father and gives His whole life in service of the Father, so too does the Father give everything to Jesus and totally commits Himself to an absolute support. Just as Jesus honors the Father, so too does the Father honor the Son. The Father gives the Spirit to Jesus "without reserve." This phrase characterizes Their whole relationship; They give Themselves to each other, "without reserve." They share a profound intimacy. Only to the Son, who abides in the heart of the Father, has the Father shown Himself fully (Jn. 1:18). And because of the nature of the relationship, it is through the Son that the Father gives Himself to others. He has entrusted to Jesus the work of reconciling the world to the Father, and has chosen to "put all things into his hands." And He never leaves Jesus alone, but is always with Him (Jn. 16:32). Just as Jesus abides in the heart of the Father, the Father abides within Jesus, and accompanies Him, works with Him, in all that He says and does, so much so that Jesus can say, "He who has seen me has seen the Father . . . I am in the Father and the Father in me . . . I do not speak on my own authority; but the Father who dwells within me does his works" (Jn. 14:9–11).

The total commitment that the Father and Son have to one another is finally and vividly expressed as Jesus gives Himself up to suffering, crucifixion and death, as the fullest possible act of abandonment in trust of the Father possible to a man. And the Father received Jesus and raises Him up from the dead and establishes Him at His right hand, restoring Jesus to the glory He had, before the world began. Jesus and the Father glorify one another, honor one another, raise one another up, out of a staggeringly profound and complete love, union and self-giving, out of a relationship that gives Them a remarkable joy, peace, confidence and security. And this is a relationship into which God desires to draw us.

As the time approaches for Jesus to give Himself completely in the crucifixion He begins to speak more directly and pointedly to His disciples about what He has been preparing them for during the previous three years. He makes clear that the relationship that they have seen Him have with His Father is a relationship that they too are being invited to enter into. Because they have joined themselves to Jesus, the Father has accepted them, taken them fully into His life and heart as sons, with Jesus, and that from hence forth they would begin to experience unfolding in their lives what it meant to be sons of God, have God as their Father.

Jesus also makes clear, that all that the Father gave to Jesus, is being given to the disciples, and that they are being called to live the same kind of relationship with the Father that Jesus lived, and have the Father work and dwell within them in the same kinds of ways. These explicit words of Jesus are so remarkable that I'd like to include a number of them at this point and have you read them carefully, paying attention to what's being said. Just as the Father identified Himself with Jesus, committed Himself to Him fully, and supported Him at every turn, dwelling within Him, so too do the Father and Jesus commit Themselves to those who have committed their lives to Jesus.

> I have said this to you in figures; the hour is coming when I shall no longer speak to you in figures but tell you plainly of the Father. In that day you will ask in my name; and I do not say to you that I shall pray to the Father for you; for the Father himself loves you, because you have loved me and have believed that I came from the Father. (Jn. 16:25–27)

> I will not leave you desolate; I will come to you. Yet a little while, and the world will see me no more, but you

will see me; because I live you also will live. In that day
you will know that I am in my Father, and you in me,
and I in you. (Jn. 14:18–20)

If a man loves me, he will keep my word, and my Father
will love him, and we will come to him and make our
home with him. (Jn. 14:23)

No longer do I call you servants, for the servant does not
know what his master is doing; but I have called you
friends, for all that I have heard from my Father I have
made known to you . . . that you should go and bear
fruit and that your fruit should abide; so that whatever
you ask the Father in my name, he may give it to you.
(Jn. 15:15–16)

Do not hold me, for I have not yet ascended to the Father; but go to my brethren and say to them, I am as-
cending to my Father and your Father, to my God and
your God. (Jn. 20:17)

In these verses (and many others) Jesus has made it clear
that His disciples are now in a direct relationship with God,
that He is a Father to the followers of Jesus just as He was
to Jesus, and that because they've followed Jesus, they've
been "born again of water and the Spirit" (Jn. 3:5) and in
the process been made "partakers of the divine nature"
(2 Pet. 1:4), sons of God, with Jesus, sharing in a direct relationship with the Father, partaking of all the possibilities
and responsibilities of sonship.

When we behold the depth of this relationship, and realize
this is precisely the relationship we are offered, we can only
pray with Paul:

I bow my knees before the Father, from whom every
family in heaven and on earth is named, that according

to the riches of his glory he may grant you to be strengthened with might through his Spirit in the inner man, and that Christ may dwell in your hearts through faith; that you, being rooted and grounded in love, may have power to comprehend with all the saints what is the breadth and length and height and depth and to know the love of Christ which surpasses knowledge, that you may be filled with all the fulness of God.

Now to him who by the power at work within us is able to do far more abundantly than all that we ask or think, to him be glory in the church and in Christ Jesus to all generations, for ever and ever. Amen. (Eph. 3: 14–21)

Knowing that we are fully sons and daughters of God, and discovering the implications of this relationship makes all the difference for living a full and fruitful Christian life. Being able to say and know *"God is my Father"* makes all the difference for prayer, love of the brethren and service to our fellow humans. Prayer is difficult for many because they have never appropriated the truths of sonship. Praying to a "God" you do not quite know is different from praying confidently and joyfully to one who you *know* loves you, cares for you, hears you, is always close, and is your Father. Genuine Christian prayer begins with the realization of being reborn into the family of God, being sons of the Father, brothers of Jesus, indwelt by God's own Spirit.

Jesus counsels His followers not to feel they must pray long and complicated prayers, but to pray simply and directly to God, "our Father . . ." When He talks to them about the need for private prayer, He tells them to go into a room alone and pray to their Father (Mt. 6:6). When the Scripture gives a picture of Jesus praying at the death of Lazarus (Jn. 11:41–42) or rejoicing in the Spirit at God's gifts to the "little ones"

(Lk. 10:21), the words "Father" are always at the heart of His prayer. Knowing God as Father is the key to Christian prayer.

Knowing God as our Father, and knowing that we're sons and daughters of God has a great influence on our relationships with other people. Many of us experience a hunger or an emptiness within. We try to fill this by looking for a certain acceptance, love, understanding and support from another person or group. When our life is not flowing from the profound peace and security that comes from knowing God's love for us as a Father, these relationships can only be frustrating and disappointing. We will be looking for something from other people that can only come from God. We can feel betrayed and become fearful and suspicious of human relationships.

God's love can free us from demanding and free us for giving in human relationships. His love can free us from possessing people. His love can let us relax and accept a relationship for what it is, without placing unreasonable demands or unrealistic hopes on it, knowing that our deepest need is filled only by God. Confidently knowing God as our Father in a profound and intimate way can free us to love and be loved without strings attached, to take disappointments with peace and to accept our own limitations with peace. We are only children together, growing into our full stature and maturity as sons and daughters of God.

Knowing God as our Father places us in a very remarkable family. We become not only brother to Jesus but to all the others who have become children of God by giving their lives to Him. This is the basis of our relationship as a Christian community, as a church. Waking up to who we are will change how we Christians relate to each other. All those who are given to Jesus are related to each other in a profound and important way, and God desires that this be expressed in active love and sharing with one another.

I couldn't help but reflect on this tonight at dinner. One of the members of our household met a priest in town visiting for a week hoping to interest University of Michigan college students in joining the missionary order of which he is a part. He placed an ad in the campus newspaper and waited in the Catholic center on campus hoping for interested students to come by. No one came. But that wasn't what struck me most about his situation. For as he went on and shared with us his weariness and discouragement, he told of how he had called two rectories in the last town he had been in asking for a place to stay and had been turned away by his "brother priests" with vague and embarrassed excuses that were rooted in the desire simply not to be bothered by a guest.

But the lack of hospitality, the lack of warmth and love evidenced in this sad happening is not untypical of life in our churches today. We have people, "brothers in Christ," stay in motels rather than in our homes all too often. And this is but a visible sign of a tragic state of Christian life.

What a contrast this was with what our house had experienced this past summer. We wanted to take a vacation as a house (several others from our Christian community live with our family) and drive from Michigan to Vermont. We asked the Lord to help us, and felt we should call some of the "brethren" in Vermont to see if they could help us find a place. We called some people in a prayer group there who immediately were able to find a good place for us to stay, in some extra rooms that a Carmelite convent had available. This in itself was a remarkable and much appreciated instance of brotherly love. But the next instances were even more striking.

We planned to break the trip into two parts, staying overnight on the way there, and on the way back, hoping to give
the children a rest. We talked about motels versus camping,
but as we talked I got a strong sense that we ought to believe
that the Christians in those towns where we would need to
stay overnight, who were experiencing a renewed life with
Christ and His Spirit, would want to receive us as brethren
into their homes. I felt almost that for Christian brotherhood
to flourish again in the Church some of us needed to believe
that those also experiencing Christian renewal in their lives
want to be brothers to us, and act accordingly. Out of the
blue, not knowing the people involved, we called some prayer
groups we had heard about and asked them if they could
provide hospitality for us. In both of the homes we stayed in,
on the way there and back we experienced the loving presence
of God in a special way as our brothers received us, and saw
also God bless them in special ways for their hospitality.

Being sons of the same Father, brothers and sisters together
means something. If we believe it and act accordingly, it can
change the face of the Church, and then the world.

Having God for our Father also has implications for how
we relate to those who are not our brothers and sisters in
Christ, to non-Christians, to our enemies, to the "man in the
street." If we have been taken up into Christ, given the Spirit
of sonship, the Father expects us to bear some family re-
semblance. He expects us to relate to all men as He Himself
does.

Christian morality flows from Christian "spirituality"—
from knowing God as our Father, and having His Spirit dwell
within us. The life of love expected of sons of God can only
come from "power from on high"—the intimate knowledge
and experience of God the Father, Son and Holy Spirit.

You have heard that it was said, "You shall love your neighbor and hate your enemy." But I say to you, Love your enemies and pray for those who persecute you, so that you may be sons of your Father who is in heaven; for he makes his sun rise on the evil and on the good, and sends rain on the just and on the unjust . . . You, therefore, must be perfect, as your heavenly Father is perfect. (Mt. 5:43–48)

Only out of the fullness of a relationship in which one is being loved, can one pour out oneself in service to our fellow men. Only when we know the person of whom we speak, can our speaking be effective in communicating the reality of that person. Whether it be helping with the physical needs of man or sharing with him the good news of salvation, knowing God as Father makes all the difference in our confidence, our joy, peace, perseverance.

In fact, I think that the almost total lack of real evangelism in many of our churches today, which is both fed by and feeds relativistic interpretations of Christianity, can be traced to a lack of genuine experience and understanding of the Father-Son relationship.

One of the most outrageous things about the Christian message and one that is widely disregarded or explained away in many of our churches is the blunt statement of Jesus: "no one can come to the Father except through me . . . I am the Way, the Truth, and the Life." What caused crowds to pick up rocks to stone Jesus was not particularly when He performed miracles, fed people, but when He identified Himself with the Father, with God Himself (Jn. 8:58, 59). The thing that shocks men about Christianity is the unique claim it makes for Christ as the way into fullness in knowledge of God. While not denying that men can come to know something of God in many ways (Rom. 1; Acts 17:22–31) Christianity makes crystal clear that the one way to entering into the fullness of life with God is through His Son Jesus. What appears to many at first sight as an arbitrary, exclusivist "doctrine" of Christianity is indeed its glory. The doctrine of the uniqueness of Christ as the way to the Father is simply pointing out the staggering fact of a God who loves more, gives Himself more, shares Himself more than men imagine. The beauty of the Father-Son relationship dispells the initial shock of the absolute statements of Jesus.

Under pressure from "enlightened" Scripture scholars and students of world religions, there are strong currents in Christianity today that make of it one of the ways to God instead of what it manifestly is, the definitive revelation of the identity of God as three persons, Father, Son and Spirit. Relativistic approaches to Christianity utterly miss the height and depth of the nature of the love of God as expressed in the Father-Son relationship. It indeed makes no sense to speak of knowing God if we don't also speak of knowing Jesus, for God is fundamentally in the depth of His being, the Father of Jesus; or of knowing Jesus without speaking of knowing the Father, for Jesus in the depth of His being is the only Son of the Father, so totally have They joined Their lives together. The witness of Their unity and love is what is intended to give hope to us who experience fragmentation and isolation in all levels of life, personal, social and political. The witness of a God that is three, and yet one, speaks profoundly to our situation, not of an annihilation of personal being, but of the fulfillment of personal being in relationship to others, through relationship to the Godhead.

Knowing that we are sons of God gives us a remarkable freedom and confidence. We can experience having no fear of "those who kill the body" because we know we are joined to God and will be with Him always. Even our bodies will be restored because we are in the hands of the Father and can count on His word. When we know that God is our Father we know that He takes care of our needs, for housing, clothing, for insight and guidance. We know we are not left orphans, that we belong to God. If we would take seriously and hold on to just one of the many words God speaks to us about His Fatherly love, what freedom would be ours from anxiety and fear, with what confidence could we live! God is eager to let us know Him in this way, and know that this is how He is to His children.

What father among you, if his son asks for a fish, will instead of a fish give him a serpent . . . If you then, who are evil, know how to give good gifts to your children, how much more will the heavenly Father give the Holy Spirit to those who ask him! (Lk. 11:11–13)

And do not seek what you are to eat and what you are to drink, nor be of anxious mind. For all the nations of the world seek these things; and your Father knows that you need them. Instead, seek his kingdom, and these things shall be yours as well. . . . Fear not, little flock, for it is our Father's good pleasure to give you the Kingdom. (Lk. 12:29–32)

I tell you, my friends, do not fear those who kill the body, and after that have no more that they can do. . . . Are not five sparrows sold for two pennies? And not one of them is forgotten before God. Why, even the hairs of your head are all numbered. Fear not; you are of more value than many sparrows. (Lk. 12:4–7)

What then shall we say to this? If God is for us, who is against us? He who did not spare his own Son but gave him up for us all, will he not also give us all things with

him? . . . For I am sure that neither death nor life
. . . nor anything else in all creation, will be able to
separate us from the love of God in Christ Jesus our
Lord. (Rom. 8:31–32, 39)

There is an utter peace, joy, security that comes from
knowing the love of God our Father. It sets us free from our
deepest fears and anxieties and lets us walk as sons of God,
confident of who we are and what we are to do, trusting in
Him who, even now, is abiding in us and working through us.
Knowing Him, and who we are, is what life is all about, is indeed, to begin already, eternal life.

CHAPTER FOUR

THE GIFT
OF THE SPIRIT

WHEN I RECOMMITTED MYSELF to Jesus, He released in me the power of His Spirit in a way similar to what the early Christians experienced. I knew a deep and profound relationship with Christ and the Father. I also felt the Spirit working in and through me in such things as prayer, sharing the good news with others, and reading Scripture. About a month after this, while alone in my room, I began to pray in sounds that I did not understand, but that seemed connected to the Lord and His Spirit. I shared this experience with a few people, and they shrugged their shoulders in bewilderment. Soon afterward I stopped praying in this way.

Two years later, when I heard that a group of Catholics in Pittsburgh had begun to experience something they called "baptism in the Spirit," I had very mixed reactions. On the one hand I felt attracted to what I was hearing. I felt it was akin to what I had already experienced, and that the Lord had something for me in it. On the other hand, I felt fearful, because I sensed that something deep within me had not yet been released to the Lord. I was afraid that if this next thing God wanted to do in my life were to take place, I might cry: I did not want to let go in that way.

There was also an element of irrational hostility in my resistance to what I was hearing about the charismatic renewal. I reacted to elements of it in ways that were clearly out of proportion to the matter itself. I later learned to recognize this "irrational hostility" reaction as a sure tip-off that the Lord wanted to do something in my life and the "old man" had sensed it and was throwing up defenses.

In some ways though I simply resented these "newly Spirit-filled Christians": I wondered why they talked as if no one had experienced anything of the Holy Spirit before them. At most, I grudgingly allowed that they might have found another way to reach what others of us had already come to. It took me several months of going through the Scripture, studying the work of the Holy Spirit, before I would even go to visit these charismatic Catholics.

The first night in Pittsburgh, in March of 1967, my co-worker, Steve, and I attended a small prayer meeting with perhaps ten people. In the middle of it, one man walked over to me and asked if I wanted him to pray for a further release of the Spirit in my life. I trusted him and what he said, and I knelt down. He laid his hands lightly on my head and began to pray.

I did not experience anything more striking of God than a sense that He was trying to do something more in my life. About an hour later this man's wife called me aside and suggested that if I just started to speak out I would pray in tongues. I did so and experienced a release of God's Spirit mingled with laughing, crying and singing as I began to pray in tongues. I suddenly remembered what I had experienced three years before and knew that I had touched home on something that God had tried to do then.

Steve and I both began to experience a new freedom in praising God. I had never before been able to pray fully the psalms of praise in the Bible, but now I suddenly found myself able to do so. I also felt the Lord moving me to pray with two people with minor physical illnesses during that next week: The illnesses cleared up.

What I experienced in Pittsburgh was not so much a great emotional event, as another significant opening of my life to God. Being willing to open up to the specifically charismatic dimensions of the action of the Spirit has proven to be a significant step in taking hold of God's promise of His Spirit. It wasn't that I hadn't experienced the action of the Spirit previous to this, for I certainly had. It wasn't even that I hadn't experienced some of the more "charismatic" workings of the Spirit before—for I had, although sporadically and somewhat mysteriously. The new element this time was a much more conscious and knowledgeable openness to the whole range of the Spirit's workings, and being supported in the expectancy of the broad range of the Spirit's action being a *normal* part of the Christian life, by a growing community of faith of which I was becoming a part.

*

In the very beginning of the Scriptures, the description of the creation, the Spirit of God moves over the face of the waters, giving life and form to the chaos. Throughout the Old Testament, that Spirit is bestowed upon certain individuals who have special roles among God's people. A deep desire takes root in the hearts of Israel for the day when God will bestow His Spirit on them all. This theme, first expressed by Moses (Num. 11:30), grows and develops throughout the Old Testament, passing from desire to a concrete and explicit promise in the prophecy of Joel:

> And it shall come to pass afterward, that I will pour out my spirit on all mankind; your sons and your daughters shall prophesy, your old men shall dream dreams, and your young men shall see visions. Even upon the men-

servants and maidservants in those days, I will pour out my spirit. (Joel 2:28–29)

In each of the four gospels, Jesus is introduced explicitly as the one who has come to "baptize in the Spirit." He will immerse God's people in the Spirit of God, in fulfillment of prophecy. Toward the end of His life Jesus began to speak more and more explicitly about the gift of the Spirit He had come to bestow. At the same time He spoke directly, for the first time of the Father, of the love and unity He intended to characterize His disciples. The link between the three is unmistakable. He even goes so far as to tell His disciples that it is better for them that He leave them physically so that they may have the Spirit. After He was crucified and had risen, His last words to his followers were:

> . . . before many days you shall be baptized with the Holy Spirit . . . you shall receive power when the Holy Spirit has come upon you; and you shall be my witnesses . . . (Acts 1:8)

They waited, they prayed. On the day of Pentecost, the Spirit came upon them in power. They spoke in tongues, praised God, and preached the message of repentance and forgiveness of sins as Jesus directed.

What Jesus had told them about, became personally experienced. They experienced a new relationship with Jesus and a knowledge of the Father, as the persons of God came to abide in their hearts through the Spirit. They experienced the persons of God working with them and in them as they preached the good news and saw the promised signs being worked in the name of Jesus. They experienced the fruits and gifts of the Spirit in genuine abundance as they moved with a new peace, joy and confidence, in who they were and what they were about, and who it was that was working with them.

Peter's sermon on that day, recorded in Acts 2, makes clear

that what the disciples were experiencing was available for *everyone*. It was to be a *normal* part of Christianity, indeed, a part of the normal experience of conversion. Subsequently, in the Acts of the Apostles, this initial outpouring of the Spirit becomes the standard expectation and experience of Christianity. Twenty-five years later, when Paul encounters a group of "disciples" at Ephesus, he asks only one question to ascertain if they are actually Christians, ". . . 'Did you receive the Holy Spirit when you believed?'" (Acts 19:2). When he discovers they did not, he tells them about Jesus, baptizes them, lays hands on them, and "The Holy Spirit came on them; and they spoke with tongues and prophesied" (Acts 19:6).

The teaching of Jesus and the experience of the early Church both explicitly point to an evident, effective reception of the Holy Spirit as the key to understanding and experiencing Jesus and the Father. They point to a clear and definite experience, of a definite Person, doing a definite work, producing definite results. Christians without such an experience were instructed and prayed with to receive it.

The Word and the Spirit of God have been active in all stages of His work with men, but there was a progressive revelation of their relationship to the Father. In Pentecost, God completed the full revelation of Himself as Father, as Son, and as Spirit. The mystery hidden for all ages was revealed, and power from it flowed forth to the ends of the earth. How does this revelation of God relate to our situation today?

Of the billion or so people who belong to the various Christian churches today, millions experience very little of what the New Testament presents as normal for Christian life. They are baptized as infants and raised in minimally Christian environments; very few are later called to an adult affirmation of their baptismal experience—a personal commitment to Christ and an effective appropriation of the power of the Holy Spirit. The rite of confirmation, intended in some churches to serve as such an adult commitment, is frequently administered in isolation from fervent Christian communities, without proper preparation and with little expectancy. In consequence, vast numbers of Christians are ignorant of the action of the Holy Spirit and so have only a dim knowledge of Jesus and the Father. If Paul were to ask them, "Did you receive the Spirit when you believed?" they, like the Ephesian "disciples," would answer, "We have never even heard of the Holy Spirit."

I'd like to share with you now part of an interview I did with Maria Von Trapp, of *Sound of Music* fame, after she experienced a release of the power of the Spirit in her life. It illuminates many of the things we're talking about.

RM: Maria, many who have read your books, and know of your dedicated Christian life, might ask themselves when they hear you've become involved in the charismatic renewal, what more could you need in your life that you didn't already have? What would you say to them?

M: Well, before we strove for perfection by the sweat of our brow, and didn't get very far. Now since being baptized in the Spirit, it's not only my own effort, but the work of the Spirit within me that is at work to make me a Christian. For example, I'm able to relate more lovingly in situations of pressure and weariness, in greeting so many people, in family relationships, than I ever could before. This is the first summer that I've been able to bear up so well under the flood of tourists who come here and want to see me. Another thing is that Scripture has become much more alive, almost as if floods of light come to me. And this is really something for I've read the Scripture all my life, but a lot of it didn't make sense to me. For example, I used to make a reverential bow to the epistles of Paul, and pass on, for I didn't understand or like him, but now the Lord really speaks to me through his writings. I can't get enough of him now. I was just reading Romans 10:1–4 and it means so much to me now.

It makes me want to approach the next bus driver or whomever I see and ask if he's been baptized in the Holy Spirit. I know I should not do things like that, but I do want to tell everyone about the gift that God has for them in His Spirit. I want them all to know this kind of happiness.

Even in living a dedicated Christian life there can be something important missing, the power of the Spirit. The apostles lived with Jesus for three years, day and night, and yet at the end of that time, something important was still missing. They hadn't yet been baptized in the Holy Spirit.

RM: How would you relate this "new Pentecost" that the Church is experiencing to the traditional Catholicism that you grew up in?

M: Well, I think the baptism in the Holy Spirit is what all Catholics ought to experience in Confirmation but don't. In Austria, and it isn't very different in America, Confirmation is a new wristwatch, a trip to the amusement park, and somewhere sandwiched in the middle, Church, "but it won't take too long." It's memorizing seven gifts, twelve fruits, fuss about a sponsor and a name, and trying to remember why the bishop is going to tap your cheek, and wondering what it's going to feel like. It's hardly ever a personally desired and experienced commitment to Jesus and release of the Spirit. Baptism in the Holy Spirit must have been the sacrament of Confirmation for the first Christians and it should be today.

RM: Do you have any thoughts about why this is the case?

M: Analyze how we Catholics grow up. We're baptized as babies, and our godparents mumble something we don't understand. We have our first confession full of *fear, and our first communion full of reverence. Some-how, somewhere, Jesus is all mixed up in this, but many of us never clearly, in words, acknowledge Him as my Savior and Lord. We may even go to daily communion all our lives and yet never have confronted the great issue of whether He is my Savior and Lord. It's not neces-sarily that we're against it—although there's usually a struggle that shows something of a reluctance when we come right down to it. Many of us have never met our Lord Jesus Christ as our personal savior.*

RM: *And yet, Maria, you would still want to say that you've been a Christian all your life, and that the Holy Spirit has been with you?*

M: *Yes, I would. But I would also want to say that there's more that the Lord has for many of us devout life-long Catholics. One of the most precious moments of my life came recently when not only was I baptized in the Spirit, but consciously and explicitly accepted Jesus as my Savior, accepting what He did for me through His death and resurrection.*

RM: *What do you mean accepting Jesus as your per-sonal savior?*

M: *Well, I know it sounds Protestant, but we have some things to learn in this area. When I first thought about doing it, it made me impatient, it just seemed like a superfluous act. And yet, a Scripture passage really helped me understand it,* Revelation 3:20–22: *"Behold I stand at the door and knock; if any one hears my voice and opens the door, I will come in to him and eat with him and he with me." I always thought, the door is open, why doesn't He come in? Of course, the door is always open, why does He have to knock? I have frequently seen a ghostly picture with Jesus knocking, but had never understood how personal, definite, and committing the invitation to come in had to be. This invitation to Him is there in many of our lives, but not consciously enough.*

We need to consciously awaken to Him and make a personal person-to-person commitment. I believe that one of the things the Holy Spirit is doing in the charismatic renewal is lifting a veil that has kept many Catholics from the personal relationship with Jesus that is there for the asking.

RM: Do you have any reflections on what the Holy Spirit is doing in the Church today?

M: I think we're involved in a direct battle between the Spirit of God and the Satanic powers. One of Satan's great triumphs is that he has gotten many priests and theologians to pooh-pooh the reality of evil spirits. When I say things like this, sophisticated young clergy say: "But Baroness, you don't believe in the devil any more do you?" This is tragic. Satan has blinded them. This is a grave mistake. We're in a battle for the world and it is our privilege and function to offer our legs, our ears, our lips, our whole beings to the sovereign Lordship of the Holy Spirit, and share with Him in this battle in whatever ways we can, big and small. I am not afraid of priests marrying or not marrying. I am not afraid of the ghastly figures that show the decline of the Church. What I am afraid of is that the Holy Spirit won't be given a chance. What we need to pray for, all of us, unceasingly, is that the Holy Spirit be given a chance. This has to happen on every level of the Church.[1]

✳

To correct this large-scale situation of impoverished Christian life, the Christian churches must proceed with a renewal and restoration of their very foundations—the process of initiation and instruction by which people enter into Christian life. In my own Church, for example, in response to the call of Vatican II, this renewal is under way. The reform of various rites, the restoration of the catechumenate for adult baptism, the beginning restoration of baptism by immersion are all hopeful signs. Also, in various places in the world, especially in parts of Latin America, infant baptism is being withheld if there is no assurance that the child will grow up in a community of faith and genuine Christian life. But this is just the beginning of a work of renewal and restoration that will take years.

And what now of the individual person seeking the power of the Holy Spirit to lead a deeper and fuller life with Jesus? How is he to proceed with the renewal of his own life while the larger renewal of the churches is in progress?

There are a number of expressions that Scripture uses for the gift of the Spirit. I have chosen to use the expression "receiving the Holy Spirit." It draws attention to an activity on our part, receiving. It is also susceptible to meaning not just the initial reception, but an ongoing receiving of the Spirit. All Christians, no matter where they are in life with Christ, have an ongoing need to receive the Holy Spirit. He is a gift given once, but also a gift that the Father and Jesus keep on giving in fuller and fuller measure.

A person seeking to receive the Holy Spirit today could easily bog down in the diversity of theological and pastoral opinion about how it is done. Some Catholics insist that the Spirit is received only in the sacraments, some evangelicals only at the moment of conversion, some pentecostals as a distinct second experience to conversion.[2] Sorting out this theological and pastoral diversity may be a work of decades. But it is already possible to find a number of theologians and pastors in almost every church expressing their experience of a fuller reception of the Holy Spirit in a way that conforms with their own tradition.[3]

For the individual person, Jesus has already shown a way to receive the Holy Spirit that cuts across all theological barriers. He has stated the only real criteria:

. . . If anyone thirst, let him come to me and drink. He who believes in me, as the scripture has said, "Out of his heart shall flow rivers of living water." Now this he said about the Spirit, which those who believed in him were about to receive . . ." (John 7:37–39)

And I tell you, ask and it will be given to you; seek and you will find; knock, and it will be opened to you. For everyone who asks receives, and he who seeks find, and to him who knocks it will be opened . . . If you then who are evil know how to give good things to your children, how much more will the heavenly Father give the Holy Spirit to those who ask him? (Luke 11:9–13)

Jesus makes startlingly clear that the Spirit is a gift for the asking. He promises it not as the reward for a life of holiness, or as a reward for a theological education, but as the initial gift that is needed for holiness and understanding—at the beginning of Christian life, not as its end.

Yet, there are obstacles that hold people back from receiving the Spirit promised by Jesus, which He yearns to give us. These are some of them.

An Intellectualized Faith

One very common problem in large segments of Christianity and in many individuals' lives is a faith that operates mainly on the intellectual level. Correct doctrinal belief is indeed of great value, but it is not the fullness of faith the Scripture talks about. The deeper question is the response of the whole person turning to Jesus with all his needs, desires, hurts, hopes. Correct belief about the Holy Spirit is by no means sufficient for receiving Him, but the hunger and thirst that longs for God and reaches out to Him in faith is. This kind of faith is something that the Holy Spirit Himself is at

work to bring about in us, even before He is able to be freely
active in our lives.

A Vague Faith

Many Christians have "faith in God," but know very little
about who this God is. They do not know what they can
sensibly have faith in Him for. In other words, their faith has
very little content. With only a vague, diffuse, general faith in
God, they are unable to ask for and receive much of what
God wants to give them. Many of us are in the same position
as the woman Jesus met at the well (John 4). We can relate
to Jesus on a certain level concerning our physical needs, just
as the woman related to Him about the physical matter of
water. If we only knew what He had to give, we would ask
and receive from Him the gift of Himself and the Father,
through the gift of the living water of the Spirit.

Problems with Sin and Guilt

If we are not willing to turn away from serious sin, we are
not able to receive the Spirit. Repentance and faith in Jesus is
a precondition. However, if we have turned from sin in our
heart and confessed it, even though we continued to struggle
and suffer falls, we can receive the Spirit. We do not have to
be perfect and sinless to receive the Spirit. It is intended as a
gift at the beginning of Christian life to enable us progressively to overcome sin in our life. Guilt is healthy if it leads us
to repent and confess, and receive forgiveness. It is not
healthy, indeed is a device of the devil to keep us from God, if
we have already repented. If we have a problem in this area
of receiving God's forgiveness and letting go of guilt feelings,
a mature Christian could probably help us, although frequently upon receiving the Spirit in greater fullness many experience an assurance of God's love and forgiveness for them.

Feelings of Inadequacy

Great numbers of our fellow human beings suffer from terrible feelings of inadequacy, particularly when it comes to relating with God. Many lay people, used to equating religion with the clergy, find it difficult to believe that God really wants to be known and loved by the "average person." A clergyman often feels a deep inadequacy precisely in spiritual matters because of his own poverty and feelings of hypocrisy. These feelings are a tremendous impediment to receiving the full relationship that the Lord wants. To both clergy and laymen God is saying, "I want you, I love you, I desire to pour out my Spirit upon you."

It will mean for many of us changing our image of ourselves and giving up our preconceptions. God is calling us all, and is more than able to help each one of us come to Him. Sometimes we believe other people can come into this relationship with God but fear that it will not happen to us. I must say quite frankly that I have never met a single person who has asked for the Spirit without eventually experiencing a full release of the Spirit in his life if he was willing to explore the possible blocks holding him back. I am convinced that no one who honestly desires to receive the Holy Spirit in fuller measure will be disappointed if he is willing to work with other Christians to remove obstacles.

Fear of What Must be Given Up

Sometimes people are prevented from receiving the Spirit by a fear of what God may ask them to give up. Sometimes it is a real fear, in the sense that God is asking them to give up some very definite thing that He considers an obstacle to the Christian life. In that case, we can expect God to help us give it up. It will hurt far less than we imagine.

More often than not, however, our fears are unfounded. We

fear that the Lord will ask us to be a missionary or not to marry or to give up all our possessions. Such fears can work deeply to hold us back from God, even cause us to run in the opposite direction. This often is the work of Satan, trying to keep us from God by exaggerating what God is asking of us. God most commonly asks us simply to open up our lives to Him. Very seldom does He ask for a "big sacrifice" right away.

I'm Not That Type

Sometimes we feel that our personality or temperament is not suited to receiving the Holy Spirit. The Holy Spirit somehow becomes associated with more outgoing personalities, a caricature perpetuated by the natural tendency of the more outgoing to dominate. From seven years' experience helping people appropriate the gift of the Spirit, I can say that the Spirit desires to work strongly in all personality types. In fact, our personalities will change. Outgoing personalities often find, upon receiving the Spirit more fully, that some of their outgoingness is brought under the Spirit's control; the shy and timid discover a new spirit of courage and confidence working within them.

False Resignation to the "Will of God"

Often people will say of the availability of more of the Spirit in their lives, "Well, whatever God wants," meaning that they do not know what God wants. They persist in praying for guidance while ignoring the guidance already given in Scripture. This attitude makes me think of Jesus asking Peter to come to Him over the water. What if Peter said, "Whatever you want Lord, I am prepared to do your will," and remained sitting in the boat, while continuing to pray for guidance and expressing his "openness" to God's will? Many of us have heard well enough to know that God is calling us to something more and desires to touch us in a new way. To persist in praying for guidance or expressing resignation to God's will is simply perverse, and is an escape tactic, subconscious though it may be.

What About Speaking in Tongues?

One of the most discussed topics today in Christianity is the whole matter of speaking in tongues. Not since the early days of Christianity has the gift been experienced in such a widespread way. Some have taken the stance that you have not received the Holy Spirit unless you speak in tongues. The action of the Holy Spirit in fervent Christians today and in other times who do not speak in tongues is ample refutation. I do believe, though, that the widespread reappearance of tongues is significant. While it is not necessary to speak in tongues in order to receive the Spirit it is a helpful thing for most people.

Speaking in tongues is presented in the New Testament as a gift of prayer. It is presented as neither the least nor the best of the gifts (Paul is not concerned with that kind of ranking). Although Paul warns us of the potential for problems in public worship, he also states explicitly that it should never be forbidden.

I believe the significance of the revival of tongues has best been pointed out by Kilian McDonnell, a Catholic researcher who has studied this spiritual renewal around the world.[4] He points out that in different cultures, religious conversion is usually characterized by some kind of bridge-burning experience, where the person who turns to God definitively steps out of the old life into the new. Even within the world-wide outpouring of the Spirit people enter into it differently in different cultures. For example, in Haiti, speaking in tongues is not particularly notable because of all the strange religious phenomena the people are used to. What is significant is that people leave behind their voodoo practices and destroy voo-doo-related objects. In Chile, on the other hand, there is a tendency to feel that unless a person has danced freely before the Lord in joy and thanksgiving he has not fully received the Spirit.

Simon Tugwell, an English Dominican theologian, points out that this link between an inner receiving of the Holy Spirit and an outward manifestation is woven throughout the tradition of the Christian East as well. He points out, for example that Symeon, the New Theologian, the greatest of Byzantine monastic reformers, "maintains that a baptism without genuine conversion is a baptism only in water. It is only the 'second baptism,' that 'of the Spirit,' which actually makes one a real Christian and a child of God, and this is brought about by a metanoia, manifested in tears [he calls it a 'baptism of tears']." Centuries earlier, Tugwell points out, "Issac the Syrian insisted also that it is only 'when you come to the place of tears' that 'you can know that you have set foot on the way of the new age.' And he specifies that it must be uncontrollable weeping, not just an odd tear or two such as anyone can wring from their eyes."[5]

McDonnell goes on to point out that most of Western Christianity is impoverished when it comes to religious experience. Through years of overintellectualization, modern man has developed a fear and resistance to religious emotion and experience. He wants to keep on top of his relationship with God and respond in carefully measured steps. Speaking in tongues is significant not only for the value of tongues in itself for prayer, but as a concrete step into a relationship with God characterized by the Spirit's freedom to act in us and a flexibility and freedom in our response.

I feel that my experience and the experience of others over the past seven years bears this out. It is not uncommon to have someone come for help in receiving the Spirit who either openly or hiddenly says, "I like this and that aspect of the work of the Spirit, but I don't want to pray in tongues." Usually this reservation indicates an attitude of wanting to keep control and not letting the reins of our life into God's hands. Although a person can receive the Spirit without speaking in tongues, there is usually an inhibition to the Spirit's working as freely as He desires until the person comes to the point where he is willing to speak in tongues. For many that is a significant stronghold of resistance to full abandonment to God. Letting go can be significant for the whole course of our life with God.

Our experience is also showing us that tongues is intended to be a basic part of a Christian's prayer life. No cure-all, but not a negligible element either. Every Christian can expect to receive this gift, and with proper instruction and encouragement from other, mature Christians, will most certainly do so.

As Tugwell puts it: "I do not believe that the Lord will refuse the gift to someone sincerely seeking it, in the full context of Christian conversion, and with a genuine desire to serve the Lord . . . Sooner or later, there must come to most Christians the challenge of the Spirit to enter into this (prophetic) inheritance. And when it comes, it may well be that the gift of tongues is the appointed doorway through which they must pass."[6]

"Do I Need to Join the Pentecostal Movement?"

No. God desires to pour out His Spirit on all flesh; you do not need to join a particular movement or denomination to receive the fullness of the Holy Spirit. Anyway, the "pentecostal movement" or "charismatic renewal" isn't a movement at all in the sense of being something you join or belong to. It is an action of God, grass roots in nature, which hopefully will disappear as a discernible movement as the whole church is renewed in the full power of the Spirit. As one of the leaders of the Catholic charismatic renewal put it, "The goal of the charismatic renewal is to disappear."

Hopefully you will be able to find a group of alive and Spirit-opened Christians right in your church, or your neighborhood, or your city, who can help you and encourage you to both open up more fully to life in the Spirit and remain a faithful and fruitful member of your present church.[7] The help and encouragement that comes from mature Christians who are more experienced in the ways of the Spirit is important. You may have noticed that a number of the obstacles that keep us back from receiving the fullness of the Spirit are best dealt with in fellowship with others who have been through them already. Being part of a prayer group that respects our present church commitment as well as the experience God is giving us, can be immensely important, even essential for growing in the life of freedom in the Holy Spirit.

We need the Holy Spirit. It is as simple as that. There is no way to know God or serve God without His Holy Spirit. We need to admit our poverty, our thirst, and let Him fill us. Again and again, more and more, we need to be filled, permeated by God's Spirit. God Himself wants to dwell within us, and work through us. His Spirit wants to rest upon us as it rested upon Jesus, guiding, teaching, comforting, interceding. And God longs to give us His Spirit; He is eager to do it. He takes delight in bestowing His Spirit.

I believe that the Holy Spirit is actually and literally "sent into our hearts, crying Father, dear Father" (Romans 8). There, in the innermost recesses of our person—our heart and will and spirit—the Spirit actually abides. There He is working to heal and impart His wisdom for a total remaking, recreating, reconstruction of our personalities. He is there educating us, nurturing us to the kingdom of the Father and union with the person of the Father, through union with

Jesus. It is the Spirit that each day is awakening our own spirit to a conscious awareness of the presence of God, an understanding of who He is, and a hunger to be one with Him.

We, in our weakness, not only do not know how to pray, but do not know how to live the Christian life, or even know who God is or want Him. It is the Spirit of God who helps us in our weakness with groans and sighs too deep for words, who is our advocate, who intercedes for us and in us and with us, who props up our weak spirits, and imparts warmth to our cold hearts.

It is He who warms us into life, loves us into truth, sharpens our sensitivity to what is in the Lord and according to his cosmic plan and what is not. He truly stands by us, our advocate.

We grow stronger, more clear-sighted, and more hungry for God Himself as He breaks up the crust of years and penetrates the hardness of a lifetime. The Father and Jesus become more vividly present to us, as their Spirit wakes us up to Their life and personal love for us, and our heart reaches out in longing for God. We feel the hurt and pain of not being with God or only being partially with Him. More and more the Spirit makes us capable of perceiving the fullness of the presence of God in Whom we move and live and have our being, and seeing how fully He is all in all.

The quality of love that exists between the Father and Son is very high. It is characterized by a profound mutual commitment, trust, tenderness and unity. It is all we mean when we call something divine, and more. It is that inner life between Father and Son that the Spirit has been given to draw us increasingly more deeply into. They are willing to accept us into Their life, and They are willing even—the marvel of it—to kneel at our feet in gentle love, and serve us, washing our feet, cleansing us, healing us, making us capable of seeing and responding. They are willing to take us, horribly deformed as we are, and gradually straighten us out again, and further, make us capable of sharing the inner life of God Himself. They are willing to sacrifice Their relationship with one another for a time, to give us a chance to share it with Them.

The Son left the heart of the Father, descended to earth in the womb of a virgin. He took upon Himself the maximum sin and hostility of the human race. He suffered disfigurement, abandonment, loneliness, voluntarily giving up the prerogatives of divinity. He went to the lowest depths, to death, to nothingness—only to rise up victorious. He blazed the way for us who would follow. He was gloriously restored to the right hand of His Father, where He is now interceding for us and pouring out His Spirit. That is what we see and hear all around us now in the new Pentecost. Around the world, that Spirit within us is even now wooing us, drawing us, calling us, to enter into the fullness of the love within God.

*

Lord Jesus, You who have come to cast fire on the earth, cast it on me. I need the fire of Your Spirit to give life to these dry bones. Breathe on me and impart to me the fullness of Your Spirit. I hunger and thirst for You; fill me with Your living water. Put me in touch with people who can help me yield to You, and unlock the power of Your Spirit within my heart.

Part Three

Prayer

CHAPTER FIVE

THE CALL TO
PERSONAL PRAYER

COMING INTO, or renewing a committed, personal relationship with the Father by acepting His Son as our Savior and the Lord of our life, and receiving or releasing the power of His Spirit within us provides the indispensable foundation for truly Christian prayer. Too many Christians are laboring over burdens in prayer that come from not having clearly established a right and full relationship with God; a relationship that isn't supposed to be the mysterious end product of a groping prayer effort, but the clear promise of God offered to Christians at the beginning of life with Him. But coming into or renewing our life commitment to Him, and receiving His power into our life is by no means the end point of our relationship with Him, but rather the beginning, however substantial and important that beginning is.

There is a thirst that leads men *into* the Kingdom, and there is a thirst that leads men *on* in the Kingdom. Many today are thirsting with the first thirst and need to turn to Jesus as their Savior and Lord and receive the initial fullness of His Spirit. But, there is a second thirst, the thirst that leads us on into the depths of the knowledge and love of God. We have partaken of His own Spirit as the completion of one process, of full Christian initiation, but this begins another process, growth in the richness and fullness of the love and knowledge of God. The Spirit has been given to us to lead us on to the heartland of the Kingdom. There is a search that leads men into the Kingdom, and there is a search that leads men on in the Kingdom. Once we have joined ourselves to Christ and drunk of His Spirit one search has come to an end, but another has begun—what the Scripture talks about as seeking the face of God.

> One thing have I asked of the Lord, that will I seek
> after; that I may dwell in the house of the Lord
> all the days of my life,
> to behold the beauty of the Lord,
> and to inquire in his temple . . .
> Hear, O Lord, when I cry aloud,
> be gracious to me and answer me!
> Thou hast said, "Seek ye my face."
> My heart says to thee,
> "Thy face, Lord, do I seek."
> Hide not thy face from me.
>
> (Psalm 27:4–9)

Paul's prayers for the early Christians were full of fervent exhortation that they would go on and know God and His incomprehensible riches, "more and more." We are not to be content at knowing His power or wisdom or mercy or love but we are to be led on by the Spirit to know Him face to face, to abound in the knowledge of Him, and to go on doing so, only more and more.

If we stop and consider how God has revealed Himself to us and notice the language of personal relationship that He uses, we cannot help but conclude that our initial or renewed commitment to Him and reception of His Spirit is intended to put us in a position where we can grow in depth in these relationships. God continually uses the language of personal relationship to reveal Himself. This language is drawn from the deepest and most intense human relationships, relationships we know so well since our whole being is rooted in them. God reveals himself as father, mother, brother, friend, husband and bridegroom. He encourages us to know Him and relate to Him in these ways. He tells us we can reliably relate to Him in these ways for this is who He is to us. Yahweh, "I am who I am," becomes progressively in salvation history, and in our lives, father and mother, brother and friend, husband, bridegroom.

This going on with God involves prayer. And prayer is simply the name that has traditionally been given to communication, conversation with God, an awareness of Him, a conscious being with Him, being present to Him, and His being present to us. Communication and conversation are essential for the development of the human relationships, the images of which God applies to Himself. In order to develop a healthy friendship, or parent-child relationship, or husband-wife relationship, a good deal of being with one another, talking to one another, just simply being aware of one another in daily life is necessary. This is also true in our relationship with God. Prayer, then, is simply paying attention to God.

Since God is similar to what we know of the human relationships images He uses of Himself, but not identical, there are some differences in how we relate to Him in contrast to how we relate to our actual husband or wife, or father or friend. The most significant one being that God is present to us, the Father and Jesus, in the Spirit. It is the Holy Spirit, sent into our hearts and spirits by the Father and Jesus, that makes Them present to us, and is the medium of our communication. The medium of our communication with the Father and Son is our heart and spirit and will and voice communicating in and with and through the Holy Spirit.

More and more the Spirit makes us capable of perceiving the fullness of God's presence in whom we move and live and have our being, and see how He truly is all in all. "Who can know a man except the spirit of that man, and who knows God except the Spirit of God, and it is that Spirit that we have received, God's own Spirit, into our innermost beings" (I Cor. 2:11–12). Prayer is that communication in the Spirit with persons whom we for the moment can't see or touch as we can our spouse or our friend or our father or mother. Yet it is truly seeing and touching of another order, and of increasing reality. Prayer is what we call the conversation and contact and communication, wordless or in words, or our deepest selves with God Himself, that happens in and through the Spirit that literally dwells within our bodies in the center of our personalities. It is the supreme importance of the person of the Spirit within us that made me take so much time in the first chapters giving witness to His work and explaining His availability. It is only when God's own Spirit is within us released and opened up to, that Christian prayer becomes an authentic possibility.

God is everywhere, always, and we can communicate with Him in the Spirit, everywhere, always. In fact, Paul commands us, "pray constantly" (I Thes. 5:17), and we ought to expect that increasingly we'll be able to pray always. Christian tradition, especially in Russian Christianity and the monasticism of the East, has attempted with real success to live out this command of Paul's, this urging of the Spirit.

Another occasion for prayer is in connection with the daily pattern of life. A traditional pattern of prayer that has helped many to a closer union with God includes prayer in the morning and evening, and prayer before and after meals. Whether the prayers are formal or spontaneous, voiced or si-

lent is not important; what is important is that they be said
attentively and in the Spirit, allowing God within us to join
in them and form them and make them sincere. In fact,
Theresa of Avila, one of the great teachers of prayer in the
Catholic tradition, claims in *The Way of Perfection* that the
sincere recitation of the "Our Father" is sufficient to raise a
Christian to the heights of prayer. Gathering together with
other Christians, whether in small groups or in church on
Sunday is also, of course, an occasion of prayer that the Lord
has encouraged and promised to bless (Mt. 18; Heb. 10).

We'll be touching on these different occasions of prayer
again, but the main kind of prayer that I'd like to consider
in this book is prayer when we're alone. Sometimes this is
called private prayer, but that communicates a sense of being
closed in on itself and out of contact with the rest of our
Christian life and brothers, and that is certainly not the case.
Sometimes it is called personal prayer, and I prefer that designation, although in no way does this imply that prayer with
others, or prayer in the official Christian assembly is imper-
sonal. I'd like to particularly consider personal prayer as I believe it is the one way of prayer most commonly neglected
today by many Christians and yet the kind of prayer that is
most centrally bound up with seeking the face of God, and
being in the kind of close union with Him that the times re-
quire.

As God reveals Himself to us by His Word and the Spirit as
father, mother, son, brother, friend, husband, bridegroom, He
also extends an invitation to let our relationship with Him
become truly intimate, close and deep. God is merciful, and
it's possible to live the Christian life, and the life in the Spirit
on any of a number of levels. There's an intrinsic dynamic,
however, in the presence of the Spirit within us and the call of

the Father, to a deeper and deeper relationship. We need to hear the gentle call of the Spirit within us to a deeper relationship and come to some decision in response. That decision, I believe for most, must concretize itself in a decision to spend some time regularly in personal prayer.

Personal relationships have laws that govern their development. Most of the laws we discover in the development of our human relationships apply also to our relationship with God. For example, in a marriage relationship it's a fact that if the husband and wife don't take some time regularly to share and communicate and just be together, their service to one another and to the children, as well as to others, will deteriorate. Just being physically present to one another or even working together on something isn't enough to sustain and deepen the relationship. The same is true in the relationship of children to their father and mother. If the family just functioned as a group all the time and there were never times when a child and one of his parents could simply be together and communicate, that deficient pattern of life would soon adversely effect the children and they would tend to withdraw, not develop quickly, and in general lose their vitality and joy.

The same is true in friendship. If two friends were friends in name and not in deed, if they never spent time together and got to know each other increasingly well, the friendship would certainly not be very supportive or satisfying.

The same laws of regularity of intimate communication apply to our relationship with God. If we don't spend time alone regularly with Him, just paying attention to Him and being with Him, not doing anything else, there will be something missing in our relationship and it will manifest itself in a variety of ways; in less enthusiasm for the Christian

life, little growth in becoming a new man, greater suscepti-
bility to sin, less power in witnessing.

The last ten years of my life have been marked by a
recognition that a daily time of personal prayer was essential
for being able to know the Lord in the way in which I sensed
Him calling me. During these years sometimes I took this
daily time in my room, sometimes in a church, sometimes
in my office. Sometimes it was just before supper or just before
going to bed, but usually it was the first thing in the morning,
before I started work. Occasionally there have been particularly busy times when I was simply unable to have time for
personal prayer, but these periods have seldom extended beyond a period of several days.

This faithfulness to a daily prayer time has made a significant difference for me in following Jesus and living the
Christian life. If, in earlier years, I missed a day or two of
prayer, it showed up in obvious ways. If I was somewhat
irritable or distant, my wife would ask, "Ralph, have you
prayed today?" My enthusiasm for the Christian life diminished, God seemed less close and personal, it became harder
to relate lovingly to people, and my desire to serve others
flagged.

As the years have passed on, God's work in me has deepened, and missing a day or two of prayer does not have such
obvious effects, but it is a tremendously important way in
which God continues to work in and through me. In fact,
I would say that the single most important decision I have
made, after turning to Christ and deciding to commit myself
to my fellow Christians, was my commitment to daily personal prayer. The trouble of working a personal prayer time
into my daily schedule has been well worthwhile.

There are a number of popular half-truths that seriously

confuse this fact for many people. For example, it is common for many to say that "all my life is prayer" or "my work is prayer." What constitutes something as prayer is that it is done with our heart and mind attuned to the Lord, in His Name. This "in His Name" isn't something that is magically tacked on at the beginning of the day in some morning offering or general intention, but is something that has to penetrate our whole being, mind, heart, spirit, subconscious functioning, in order to be truly effective in making worship of everything we do. Our whole life and our work can and should be a prayer, an act of adoration and thanksgiving and offering to God but they are not that simply by declaring them so. Prayer, as with salvation, doesn't come by changing our language. It comes by death to self, minute by minute, fidelity and obedience, and for most of us, only through times of personal prayer. Personal prayer isn't all of prayer and isn't supposed to be. But I have never met anyone, in centuries past in Christian literature or today in my own experience, who has effectively succeeded in having their whole life and work as genuine worship without definite time spent in regular personal prayer.

In a mature and unusually blessed marriage relationship or friendship, the persons involved *may* be able to go for days on end with unbrokenly being present to one another and in profound communion without taking time to specifically spend together, but it is very rare if at all possible and certainly not indefinitely. And yet that is the relationship of union and communion that people feel they can have by declaring it so rather than facing the solid truth of what's necessary for personal relationships of that sort to develop.

Another half-truth that blocks people from seeing the need for personal prayer is a fixation with the liturgy or Eucharist, which sees it not only as the theological and worship "summit of Christian life" but as the "sum" of Christian life, admitting no other prayer expressions as important or essential. The Eucharist or Lord's Supper is indeed a central part of Christian life, but it isn't the totality of it. Furthermore, what it is in theological fact, it seldom is in practical effect. What the Christian people are not living and expressing outside of the Eucharist they cannot live and express inside it. If people are not living in deep union with God outside of the liturgy in their daily lives when they come together to celebrate the Lord's death until He returns, there will be precious little celebrating, and that is certainly the situation today. So many have placed their hopes on liturgical reform and renewal in bringing about a renewed church, but liturgy can't express something that isn't there. What is needed in the Church is a fundamental and direct evangelism to draw people to a personal commitment to Jesus as Lord and Savior, and to invite them to a release of the power of the Spirit in their lives. Then celebration, praise and worship of the whole heart and whole man becomes possible. Then, liturgy can become what Jesus means it to be. But even then, such eucharistic celebration can never be the exclusive point of prayer. If a human family only got together to celebrate once a week at dinner, or even once a day, something would be missing in those relationships and those celebrations.

Jesus gave a strong and direct call for personal prayer in word and example, as well as a call to communal and eucharistic prayer. All are needed for the full relationship with Him, that He desires. Jesus, who had the most intimate relationship with the Father possible and the most unbroken communion, except when it was willingly sacrificed as He tasted desolation and death for us, set a conspicuous example of slipping away to spend time alone with the Father, even whole nights, and directed His followers to do the same. We see also, how He desires those following Him to be close to Him, to give Him support and personal friendship.

When you pray go to your room and close the door and your Father who hears you in secret will reward you. (Mt. 6:5)

Could you not watch with me one hour? (Mt. 26:40)

The decision to enter into the deeper relationship with Him that is being offered must involve the decision to spend time regularly, daily, in personal prayer. In order for the decision to be effective, it has to be concretized as to time and place. In fact, wisely choosing the time and place is usually a process that takes awhile to be satisfactorily concluded, and is itself half the battle.

Finding the right time is going to take some thought and some consultation with those we live and work with. Generally, it seems best to choose a daily time for personal prayer as one of the first things in the morning: For some, however, this is not desirable or possible. For some, scheduling the prayer time into the lunch hour seems to be best; for others, some evening hour; for some, the hour must vary from day to day, but if a daily prayer time is not scheduled for each of these days, it almost certainly will not happen regularly, if at all. A real estate man I know gets up early in the morning to pray; an aero-space engineer prays and reads Scripture on his lunch hour; a production manager of a computing firm prays after the children are in bed at night.

The multiplicity of demands on our time and attention is such that if we do not put a priority on spending time alone with the Lord each day we are not likely to do it. Some have a reluctance to schedule because it seems "unspontaneous." But if we consider any other important relationship, we realize that when it becomes serious it passes from the spontaneous (and haphazard) to the committed and scheduled. If two people want to become more than mere acquaintances, they need to agree on definite times and places to get together. If parents of a growing family want to regularly spend time together, they must schedule it, plan on it and arrange for baby-sitting. Romantic ideas about spontaneity are just that: romantic and not realistic. There is plenty of room for spontaneity within the framework of a committed relationship with regular times scheduled to be spent together. There can be extra times together, unplanned and spontaneous. There can be spontaneity within the regular times. But if there is no base of committed regular time together, there is not going to be much of a relationship. There may have been another age and time when the multiplicity of demands and sensory over-load was not such as it is today (there may not have been, either!); but today if we do not make commitments and guarantee their fulfillment by scheduling time for them, we allow our life to be ruled by whomever or whatever grabs us first. That is frequently not the Lord. A schedule that works is a gift from the Lord, and an expression of His wisdom and love. Taking time to carefully work one out as regards personal prayer (as well as our other important responsibilities) can do a great deal to solidify our relationship with Him. If your first schedule does not work, do not become discouraged. It is well worth working on the right one for years, if necessary; it is that important.

Finding the right place is also important, although not usually quite as difficult as finding the right time. It should be a place where we are comfortable (not too hot or cold); a place without a lot of distractions; a place where we will not be interrupted; a place where we can sit or stand or walk or kneel, as the Spirit may lead us; a place where we can sing or dance as well as remain silent. If the ideal place does not exist, get the best you can, and God will honor it.

As seemingly mundane as considerations of time and place are, working them out satisfactorily can solve a lot of spiritual problems.

✳

Some feel that any question of method is irrelevant when the Holy Spirit has been released in their lives. They feel that prayer "comes naturally" and there is no need for instruction. Most people, however, even though they are experiencing a renewed or new life with God in the Holy Spirit, run into problems and questions in prayer and are not satisfied with their progress. Half the battle, but only half, is regularizing the daily time and place of prayer. Many other problems flow from ignorance of how to spend a profitable prayer time. Most people by temperament and natural ability are not capable of, or easily interested in, the rigorously constructed systems of meditation that earlier generations were raised on. With the fuller release of the Holy Spirit in people's lives, the same rigor is not always quite appropriate or even helpful.

I would like to suggest a prayer time with a simple structure that allows a great deal of variety and response to the Spirit's leadings, yet gives enough form so that one is not at a loss when times of dryness come. This kind of structure comes naturally to some, but by no means to all. Even those praying in this way spontaneously can find help in becoming conscious of what they are doing and why, both for the inevitable days of testing ahead, and to learn to share their good fortune and help others into a regular life of personal prayer.

Spiritual Reading

It is the united witness of Christians from all centuries that personal prayer should be supported by regularly reading

Scripture and other books that reveal something of God and give us a desire to know and love him more. Spiritual reading is not necessarily study. It does not aim at knowing for the sake of knowing, or knowing for the sake of doing something. In one sense anything can serve to draw us closer to God, and it has become fashionable to talk about the daily newspaper as our spiritual reading. The newspaper may occasionally or secondarily perform that function, but that is not its primary purpose. Prayerfully reading the Scriptures, listening for the word of the Lord, is spiritual reading. Reading the biography of a great man or woman of God, with the primary purpose of learning how to serve God better and love him more, and being inspired to that end, is spiritual reading. Reading about collegiality in the Church or the formation of parish councils, or the scholarly attempts to sort out the diverging resurrection narratives, while helpful and important, are not spiritual reading in the sense we are using.

When people speak about their "prayer time," they are often referring to the time they spend in spiritual reading as well as in prayer. Since the two are so closely related, this is an acceptable way of speaking if we are clear about how the two work together and the distinction between the two. The danger, of course, in associating the two so closely under the title of "prayer time" is that we may spend more of the time reading and thinking that we are praying. Let us for our purposes accept the designation "prayer time" as referring to both our spiritual reading and our explicit prayer and see how they can work together.

An ancient method of prayer and spiritual reading consists in slowly and prayerfully reading a passage from Scripture, pausing again to let prayer develop from that, alternating for the whole prayer time. The regularity of the reading guards from distractions, and the freedom to move to prayer as the

Spirit leads gives the necessary freedom. It is a method of working prayer and spiritual reading together that many have found helpful and that has produced real holiness. Abbot Marmion, one of the early twentieth century's most vital interpreters of the classical tradition of prayer, as well as one of the trail blazers in a new emphasis on the Holy Spirit, has this to say about this method of prayerful reading:

"For the monk, mental prayer is nothing else than these pauses in the reading of Holy Scripture or pious books, during which the soul raises itself to God, unites with His will, and in His sight discovers its faults and God's designs for it. St. Benedict says that in general these pauses must be "short," unless the grace of the Holy Spirit prolongs them, but as soon as the movement of grace leading us to unite ourselves to God ceases, we must resume our reading or the recitation of the psalms. This was the only mental prayer known and practiced by those giants of holiness, the Fathers of the desert, and the monks of the West merely contined this tradition. The simple way of the monks of old produced so many contemplatives and so many saints. This method has the advantage of being within the reach of everyone, and to lessen the number of distractions, and as it has raised thousands of souls in the past to the highest contemplation, it can lead us, too, to this same grace."[1]

Another way of combining spiritual reading and prayer would be to spend the first half of our prayer period in spiritual reading, and the second half in prayer, or vice versa. This would allow a fuller development of the prayer response in praise, worship, petition, silence or whatever.

If we have a prayer time of a half hour, fifteen minutes could be devoted to spiritual reading, fifteen to prayer. If we have an hour prayer time, half an hour could be devoted to reading, half to prayer. This is a good rule of thumb but it should be considered a rough guide rather than a law. Some days we may spend our whole prayer time in prayer, depending on how the Spirit is leading. Some people may regularly spend less time reading than praying. I would doubt the wisdom of spending the whole time in reading, except on very rare occasions. The danger is that spiritual reading becomes a substitute for prayer. It is imperative that whatever method we use we put the book down and turn to the Lord directly! Reading is an aid, not a substitute.

While I've been talking about reading as an aid to prayer, many today are finding listening to cassette tapes on spiritual subjects an effective supplement to prayer as is spiritual reading.[2] Whether we're a "book person" or a "tape person," a regular source of spiritual nourishment can greatly aid our prayer life.

I am not prepared to suggest an order in which the different elements of prayer should occur in our prayer times—vocal praise first, then silent adoration, etc. But I would like to indicate some of the elements that should be regularly represented in our prayer, not because we decide they should be represented, but because they are things the Spirit regularly strives to do in each of us.

Praise

Frequently the Spirit strives to move us to praise. One of the outstanding characteristics of the charismatic renewal, one of the main effects of the baptism of the Spirit is that it releases in us a Spirit of praise of God. I have heard countless people testify to the way they praised God from their hearts for the first time. Prayers of praise are found throughout the

Scriptures and our liturgical services, but how seldom are they prayed from the heart. Glory to God for the freedom to praise Him! It is good to praise the Lord even when we do not feel like it; feelings sometimes follow our praising from our will. Sometimes beginning to pray in tongues can free in us the Spirit of praise and worship.

Praise can be silent or vocal. Oftentimes I find it helpful to walk around my office where I pray, clapping my hands and singing. Singing in tongues is a great way of praising God that the Spirit gives.

Just recently a remarkable article appeared in my office at *New Covenant* from a writer describing his research into early Christian worship. In it he indicated that spontaneous singing (and dancing) in the Spirit was a regular part of Christian worship into at least the beginnings of the seventh century. In reading some of the descriptions of this worship that he provided, I couldn't help but notice their remarkable similarity to the restoration of "singing in the Spirit" as found in the renewal today.[3]

Freedom in expressing our praise to God is important; scarcely ever will it be exactly the same as it was the day before. I would think that every day in our prayer time we should have some time of praising the Lord, whether we feel like it or not. I would suspect that there will be prayer times when that is all we will do the whole time—we will not even have time for reading. How good God is, how good it is to praise Him!

Silent Adoration

Sometimes after praising the Lord, or before or during, it seems right just to be silent and aware of the Lord's presence. It is good to be silent before the Lord. Sometimes that is what the Spirit is doing in us. To try to pray out loud at that time would be grieving Him. Sometimes we may be silent for the whole prayer period, not in the dead silence of vacuity, or sleep, but in the full silence of awareness of Him.

For God alone, my soul waits in silence. (Psalm 62:1)

Be still and know that I am God. (Psalm 46:10)

Recently I had an experience that remarkably illustrated how the Spirit leads us at times simply to be still and know that He is God. I had come into work in the morning and wasn't feeling very well at all. I had a headache and felt nauseous. Yet I knew I should attempt my regular prayer time anyway. But the sound of voices in animated conversation from adjoining offices made it almost impossible to concentrate, on top of feeling ill, so I went to a nearby storeroom and brought in a chair to sit and pray. But I could hardly hold my head up straight it hurt so much, so I leaned forward on to a carton and just rested it there. I could scarcely think straight for the tiredness and the pain but somehow deep in my being I tried to turn to God and just point in His direction, as it were. As I did so, I began to sense that He was there, that He was coming to me and filling me up. In a few minutes, as I held very still, increasingly aware of Him, not moving, or able to say words, not really having the strength to pray, He seemed to comfort me with His Spirit and presence and in a few more minutes the pain had gone away, the headache and nausea was gone, the tiredness was gone, and I was able to joyfully praise Him and sing in the Spirit. This has happened before and since, and it seems to be one of the ways the Lord teaches me about holding still and being silent, and letting Him be God.

Conviction

Sometimes the Spirit will cause us to become aware of something in our life that He wants us to take note of. Sometimes He uses our prayer time to make us aware of something that is not right. Perhaps an offense against a brother that we must make right. Perhaps a fundamental thing that pervades our life and is hard to see because we are so much involved in it. Perhaps something that needs to change in our priorities or schedule, or something that needs to change in our relationship to our wife or children or co-workers. The Spirit is striving to bring forth in us the fullness of the new creation and will be showing us things that need to be changed. We must be open to this work of His. Sometimes take some time in prayer just to ask Him to show you things, and consider your life before Him, asking for light.

A few years ago, for example, I was praying and I began to have a strong sense that I ought to reflect on my relationship with my wife. The particular area was an area in which I was frequently impatient with her. I felt the Lord was giving me a sense, through His Spirit, that it was never helpful or loving to be impatient in the particular situation, and that I needed to resolve not to respond like that again. That made a major difference in my response in certain situations and resulted in a real change. Things like that periodically happen, and we need to be alert and listen when the Lord speaks to us like this.

Intercession

The Spirit will lead us in our prayer to pray for needs that we and others have. Sometimes our whole prayer time will be taken up with this. At other times, the Spirit will not let us intercede, but directs us simply to praise. We will be saying more about intercession in a later chapter.

Revelation

Sometimes the Spirit will reveal to us a new insight into Christian truth, something about the crucifixion or the second coming, or the forgiveness of sins, or our Father, or about Himself. It may come from reading, it may come directly in prayer; we should let it come, receive it, mull over it, let it bring life to us. Truths given in this manner are a special work of the Holy Spirit and make more difference in our lives than several theology courses on the subject. The Spirit, as Jesus promised, will lead us into all truth, and recall and make vivid to our minds what Jesus has said. Carry this new truth around with you all day, and all night, and all week; rejoice in it, thank God for it, share it with others.

I recall a few months before getting married, sitting on the floor in my room praying and getting a distinct sense that the Lord was showing me that my life from now on needed to be based on perfect unity with Him and perfect unity with my wife. He gave me a clear sense that this was to be the basis out of which my life would be fruitful. Since then I've found this "revelation," which is how I experienced it, bearing very good fruit in my life and proving to be absolutely true.

I remember also a few months before that, sitting on the same floor praying, and thinking over a talk I was going to give to some college students on the basic Christian message, when all of a sudden the Spirit began to give me a new understanding of the Trinity; the "revelation" of which has continued to be very important in my personal life and how I experience God.

I believe the Lord wants to reveal truths about Himself and ourselves to all of us. We need to be prepared to "pay attention" when His Spirit begins to "lead us into all truth" (Jn. 16:13).

Rejoicing

Rejoicing can be a part of the elements of prayer already mentioned, particularly praise, but it also can be a distinct prayer of its own. Being glad about what God has done, what God is doing, what God will do, who He is, and His mercy to us, is a form of prayer and is to be yielded to freely. Sometimes I walk around my office just rejoicing and thanking and praising; sometimes I walk down the street rejoicing. This is what Saint Paul tells us to do, not because it is a good idea but because we have every reason to "rejoice always." That is what the Spirit sometimes enables us to do in a special way in prayer.

> In that same hour he rejoiced in the Holy Spirit and said, "I thank thee Father, Lord of heaven and earth, that thou hast hidden these things from the wise and understanding and revealed them to babes; yea, Father, for such was thy gracious will. All things have been delivered to me by my Father; and no one knows who the Son is except the Father, or who the Father is except the Son and any one to whom the Son chooses to reveal him." (Lk. 10:21–22)

The method of personal prayer that I am suggesting is very simple. It involves a simple understanding of prayer and reading, and a reasonably balanced, although not absolute, framework for using them together; a reasonable understanding of the variety we can expect to experience in prayer; and a reliance on the Holy Spirit to lead us to the length and manner of prayer that is best at a particular time. The Spirit blows where He wills, but it helps to have our bearings.

CHAPTER SIX

PRAY, AND DO NOT
LOSE HEART

Anyone who has tried to pray has at one time or another found it difficult.

"I'm not experiencing the presence of God. I feel like I'm talking to a blank wall. God seems absent."

"I'm distracted constantly. I seem restless, preoccupied."

Unfortunately, the difficulties, while normal and to be expected, can seriously block our relationship with the Lord. Many who set out on the way to a deepening personal relationship with God have turned back because of them. With modest courage and understanding, however, we can get through these difficulties if the right help and encouragement is available. I want to consider some of the common problems that people experience, and ways we can work them through.

Dryness

Dryness is perhaps the most common difficulty. Whether one week, one month, or one year after initial conversion or renewal, it is almost certain to come. Dryness consists in not experiencing the presence of God or the desire to pray. God may seem absent or distant; we may feel we are talking to ourselves. It becomes more difficult to persist in prayer under such circumstances; yet if understood correctly, these can be special times of grace.

Experience of God is intended to be a normal part of the Christian life. It is not, however, without its variations. Sometimes our failure to experience God in a sensible manner comes through no fault of our own, but is a normal stage in God's purification of our desire and intention to serve and follow Him. When we experience His presence in a satisfying way, our feelings may well become the motive for our love of Him. Love will not mature or deepen unless it reaffirms its choice of the Beloved when the consolation of experience is not there.

Some dry times are caused by normal fluctuations in our human nature. Our psychological and physical well-being will inevitably affect our experience of God. Lack of sleep or food (or too much) can affect our prayer times, as can the psychological drain of long sustained efforts. We should not be alarmed at these effects but should seek God for the wisdom we need to deal with the root problems.

God's plan for us is ultimate union with Him. Our experience of God will deepen as our fidelity through dry times remains steady. Temptations to shorten our prayer times during these periods, or to drop them altogether, should be resisted. Getting out of the habit of regular prayer prolongs the dry time, and makes it more difficult to respond to the next prompting of the Holy Spirit.

Trials—Suffering

Our progress in prayer may also be interrupted when we become involved in difficult or painful situations. Much of what was said about dryness applies here. We are warned in Scripture that we will not be magically spared trials and sufferings as Christians; indeed, we are told that God often permits trials to bring about the steadfastness and seriousness of character that he wants us to have (James 1:2–4). Someone who has committed himself to God, and loves Him, can be assured that God will bring great good out of everything that happens (Rom. 8:28). The very force of the trial or suffering, if we look on it with hope and faith, can be turned to produce a comparably strong good.

Let me make a few distinctions, however. There are some trials that God does not intend us to accept in faith but to resist and overcome: sufferings coming from our own sin or a wrong situation or an attack of Satan. Things that we bring on ourselves or have control over we should repent of, resist or change. It is not God's will that we experience them.

> Submit yourselves therefore to God. Resist the devil and he will flee from you. Draw near to God and he will draw near to you. Cleanse your hands, you sinners, and purify your hearts, you men of double mind. (James 4: 7–8)

There are trials—the loss of a job, for example—that may indeed be attributed in some way to Satan but are to be borne in faith. God will bring good out of them.

The main kind of suffering spoken of in the Scriptures comes from the attempt to follow Christ faithfully. It is the suffering of death to self and the daily carrying of the cross: the persecution and inconvenience that are encountered; the sacrifices that must be made; the misunderstanding that must be endured. It is a suffering that is to be borne joyfully and counted as a normal part of our life.

> Beloved, do not be surprised at the fiery ordeal, which comes upon you to prove you, as though something strange were happening to you. But rejoice in so far as you share Christ's sufferings, that you may also rejoice

and be glad when his glory is revealed. If you are re-proached for the name of Christ, you are blessed, because the spirit of glory and of God rests upon you. But let none of you suffer as a murderer, or a thief, or a wrong-doer, or a mischief-maker; yet if one suffers as a Christian, let him not be ashamed, but under that name let him glorify God. (I Peter 4:12–16)

Regularity of Prayer Time

We may have difficulty experiencing God because we are skipping our prayer time or letting it get pushed out of our schedule. I cannot overemphasize the importance of faithful-ness and regularity; they significantly reduce many of the problems people experience in trying to pray. We usually need the support of other people encouraging us to take our prayer time and not asking us to do other things at that time. It may appear Christian to yield to every demand, even when it consistently prevents us from praying, but it is not. We cannot ignore the consequences to our long-range com-mitments: Saying yes to every immediate demand can amount to saying no to God. It injures others in the long run for the need of the moment. We can become bound up by what has been called the "tyranny of the urgent." We need not be "rigid" in any part of our Christian lives, and must always be ready to help a brother or sister in need even if it interferes with our prayer time, but we need also to have God's own wisdom and to know that to choose a life of personal prayer, to choose to be faithful to our daily prayer time (making allowances for legitimate exceptions), is to be choosing the pearl of great price, the treasure in the field, is to be choosing God Himself.

At the same time, our prayer time should not be completely inflexible. We should not feel that God will not love us if we miss an occasional prayer time (or all our prayer times for that matter!), but His love desires the best for us and our brothers. That is why we pray. Also, it is possible, of course, to use our prayer time as a means to hurt other people or shirk our responsibilities. A parent who schedules his prayer time for the hour after supper, when several children need to be put to bed and the service of both parents is required, will only cause hurt and resentment. The solution is not to give up our prayer time, but to find a better time. In families, parents should work out their personal prayer times in light of each other's needs, to their mutual satisfaction. It may take a while to hit on the right time, but keep trying!

Length of Prayer Time

We may experience difficulty in prayer because we have committed ourselves to a prayer time that is too long or too short. If too long, it becomes a strain and a burden; if too short, it will not allow for all that the Holy Spirit wants to do in us. Something between the time we pray on our best days and the time we pray on our worst days is probably right. If we are just beginning to pray, it would be good to be conservative, taking perhaps ten to fifteen minutes a day for the whole prayer period, including some spiritual reading. We can increase it gradually to a half hour, and perhaps eventually to an hour.

Lack of Peace—Restlessness—Preoccupation

Indications of lack of peace, restlessness, and preoccupation are sometimes closely related, and we will deal with them together here. There are a number of things that can cause these obstacles.

SIN AND GUILT

Unconfessed sin can choke off our prayer. When we do something wrong, we ought immediately to confess to the Lord, repent of it, and firmly resolve not to repeat it. We can be assured of Christ's forgiveness when we confess our sin, and we should not allow guilt to plague us or quench our prayer. There is no place for guilt in the Christian life except as a sign that we need to confess to the Lord.

Blessed is he whose transgression is forgiven,
whose sin is covered.
Blessed is the man to whom the Lord imputes no iniquity,
and in whose spirit there is no deceit.
When I declared not my sin, my body wasted away
through my groaning all day long.
For day and night thy hand was heavy upon me;
my strength was dried up as by the heat of summer.
I acknowledged my sin to thee, and I did not hide my
iniquity; I said, "I will confess my transgressions to the
Lord"; then thou didst forgive the guilt of my sin.
(Psalms 32: 1–5)
If we confess our sins, he is faithful and just, and will
forgive our sins and cleanse us from all unrighteousness.
(I John 1:9)

WRONG RELATIONSHIP

Jesus' directives for our relationships are clear. We are to continuously forgive others and not hold any resentment against them, forgiving as He Himself forgives. In fact, He taught us to ask Him to forgive us as we forgive others. He told us to turn back from worship if there is anything wrong between us and our brothers and set that right first (Mt. 5:23–24). To a startling degree, problems in this area are a hindrance to joy and peace in prayer. The lack of peace is a signal that we need to take care of the problems.

Sometimes, on the conscious level things may seem "in order," but often there can be deeply buried hurts and resentments that effectively prevent that peace with God from developing out of which prayer flows more easily. It is not uncommon for the Holy Spirit over a period of time to open up these deeply buried areas and allow us to finally and freely give forgiveness to someone who has hurt us, or heal some wound inflicted long ago; from as long ago even, as earliest childhood. If we feel that there may be some deeply buried hurts blocking our relationship with God, we can invite the Holy Spirit to bring these to the surface, or perhaps pray with an experienced Christian for "inner healing."[1]

Some relationships we should not be in at all. For example, a married man should not develop a close, dependent relationship with a woman other than his wife. A person committed to celibacy should not get involved in such a relationship either. Unless our relationships are right, our prayer can be hindered.

LACK OF ORDER IN OUR LIFE, "BUSYNESS":

If we have not established a basic order among our various responsibilities and are "running around like a chicken with its head cut off," we can be sure that our prayers will be hindered. Our home life, work life, free time and friendships must be working right, or on their way to working right, if our prayer time is to work right. We may be doing too many things, or we may be doing things in a helter-skelter way. Both produce a sensation of chaos which is an obstacle to prayer.

Some people who say they have no time to pray actually have plenty of time, but have managed and invested it badly.

Sometimes they do not really know how they are spending their time. Here we again see the value of a schedule. We need to sit down and see what we are doing and when we are doing it, and then evaluate what we should do and when we should do it. It helps to write everything down, not forgetting time for traveling from place to place, eating, reading mail, putting the children to bed, washing dishes. Then we can figure out which things are most important, giving a high priority to personal prayer. We can schedule these things and work with that schedule for a while, expecting to make adjustments before it works well. We may have to revise it periodically as circumstances change. Making a workable schedule is an art that requires much practice and involves many mistakes, but is one well worth learning.

Some people are doing too much and need to slow down. We must have enough breathing space and leisure to allow a spirit of prayer to develop and permeate our whole life. Making decisions about our job and where we live, our friends and our activities, with an eye to their effect on our ability to spend time with the Lord and maintain a basic sense of peace, is very important.

"Psychic overload"—having too much going on, too much to think about—is one of the commonest causes of difficulty in prayer. The only cure is to put some order into our life, possibly do less and clear out some peaceful time to be with the Lord. Even with a good time for personal prayer, if the rest of our life is too intensely packed with activities, we are likely to remain preoccupied while praying.

ANXIETY

The Scripture contains some clear instructions about anxiety. Jesus told his disciples, ". . . do not seek what you are to eat and what you are to drink, nor be of anxious mind. For all the nations of the earth seek these things, and your Father knows that you need them" (Lk. 12:29–30). Paul exhorted the Philippians to "Have no anxiety about anything, but in everything by prayer and supplication with thanksgiving, let your requests be known to God" (Phil. 4:6). If we do not obey these instructions, anxiety will undercut our prayer. It will take some time to learn how to give our anxiety over to Him, but the lesson must be learned if we are to move forward with the Lord. "Cast all your anxiety on him, for he cares about you" (I Peter 5:7).

SLEEPINESS

If we are sleepy, we should consider whether we are getting enough sleep, rest and exercise.

Occasionally a spirit of sleep can plague us, and it ought to be resisted and rebuked in the name of Jesus.

Sometimes it helps to change our prayer posture and begin to pray more actively, perhaps standing or walking around and praying out loud or singing.

Praying or singing out loud, and walking around while we're praying, can in fact make fruitful a prayer time that could have easily been short-circuited by sleep or distractions.

Distractions

Superficial distractions, as opposed to more deep-rooted problems arising from lack of organization, can be handled in a number of ways.

Some can be incorporated into our prayer. For example, if we are thinking of somebody in our prayer, we can pray for them. If we are concerned about some situation, we can turn it over to the Lord and move on to other things. Things we "remember to do" while praying can be jotted down quickly on a nearby pad for later reference, and we can go on in prayer freed of the anxiety of forgetting.

Some distractions must simply be endured and made the best of: the noise of pneumatic drills when the street is under construction, for example.

Some distractions can be eliminated by taking specific action. For example, I always found it very distracting to see a pile of messages, memos, and correspondence waiting on my desk when I arrived at the office and took my prayer time. I solved that by asking my secretary to hold them until I finish praying. Another serious distraction was the telephone, so I asked that telephone calls be held until I finish praying, unless there is an obvious emergency. We have not really had one of those in many months. It is important that we not be slaves to the phone or mailman or whatever. A peaceful and uninterrupted prayer time makes quite a difference in our ability to pray.

Some distractions need to be dealt with vigorously and resisted. Letting our mind wander or daydream can sometimes only be successfully dealt with by vigorous resistance. There is an undeniable element of crucifying the flesh involved in the Christian life, and unless we have the courage to endure the pain of self-denial when appropriate we will not make much progress. But God is faithful and He will give us the courage we need. In fact He probably already has. Use it.

CHAPTER SEVEN

THE NEED FOR OTHERS

V ERY RARELY is a human being able to grow in union with God without considerable help and support from others. The most many can manage is a kind of holding action—not moving forward, but desperately clinging to whatever relationship with God they already have. I, personally, know that it has only been through the support and encouragement of other Christians that I have been able to go on with the Lord as I have. God wants each Christian to have the support of brothers and sisters.

Many of my fellow Catholics have at one time or another tried to lead a life that included personal prayer but found themselves unable to sustain prayerful meditation on the Word of God on their own. They frequently gave up their belief that God was calling them into a deep personal union with Himself, or at least they doubted their ability to respond and persevere.

Those who have given up in the attempt to respond to the call of God, "deep calling to deep" as concretized in a life of personal prayer, could have, and can, be helped immeasurably by the immense support that comes from being a part of a vital and active Christian community.

In fact, I think that most of the weight placed on private

meditation in parts of the Catholic tradition of prayer was effectively being borne, in early Christianity, by the vitality of the interaction in the early communities. The vitality of their common life together enabled the Word of God to be spoken in a rich variety of forms, interwoven with the fabric of daily life. Some of these forms, such as prophecy, for example, had, and have today, extraordinary meditative power. Their life and worship together was, from what we can tell, far more effective in producing both contemplative awareness of God's presence in daily life and in practical changes in their life.

> And do not get drunk with wine, for that is debauchery; but be filled with the Spirit, addressing one another in psalms and hymns and spiritual songs, singing and making melody to the Lord with all your heart, always and for everything giving thanks in the name of our Lord Jesus Christ to God the Father. (Ephesians 5:18–20)
> What then, brethren? When you come together, each one has a hymn, a lesson, a revelation, a tongue, or an interpretation. (I Cor. 14:26)

I think it is clear from Scripture that God's fundamental intention is not that we approach union with Him and a life of prayer as our personal burden, but rather as a concern shared by the community of which we are a part. God's plan for our approach to Him is essentially communal. As we open up to the Holy Spirit we need to open up to being drawn from what for many of us is a highly individualistic form of life to an increasingly community-oriented form of life. As our commitment to Him grows, His intention is that our commitment to one another grows. As we love Him more and more His intention is that we love one another more and more. Loving God and loving our neighbor are, for a Christian, part of the same call.

If any one says, "I love God," and hates his brother, he is a liar; for he who does not love his brother whom he has seen, cannot love God whom he has not seen. And this commandment we have from him, that he who loves God should love his brother also. (I John 4:20–21)

When the Holy Spirit is given He is given not just to bring us into a personal union with God, but into a new relationship with one another. When He was given on the day of Pentecost, we see that one of the main results was a change in the relationships of the early Christians with one another. They moved, definitively, into a community way of life where they cared for one another and shared their lives together, experiencing themselves as members of one family, "brethren" together.

And fear came upon every soul; and many wonders and signs were done through the apostles. And all who believed were together and had all things in common; and they sold their possessions and goods and distributed them to all, as any had need. And day by day, attending the temple together and breaking bread in their homes, they partook of food with glad and generous hearts, praising God and having favor with all the people. And the Lord added to their number day by day those who were being saved. (Acts 2:43–47)

The experience of God's love being poured into their hearts through the Spirit freed them from the fears, pride, resentments that kept them apart, and drew them into a relationship with one another as brothers and sisters that was expressed in countless practical ways.

Most kept their regular occupations. Although the Jerusalem community actually pooled their financial and material resources, other communities accomplished this resource sharing in more informal ways. But what characterized all the early Christian communities we have record of was a community style of life that embodied real and frequent contact with one another and care for and encouragement of one another.

But is it any surprise that a God who is a union of three persons, communal in His essence, would create the human race for community, and in the redemption of that race call them out of their isolation back into community? Jesus' prayer shortly before His crucifixion expresses the depth of God's desire for union with us and desire for us to be in union with one another.

I do not pray for these only, but also for those who believe in me through their word, that they may all be one; even as thou, Father, art in me, and I in thee, that they also may be in us, so that the world may believe that thou hast sent me. The glory which thou hast given me I have given to them, that they may become perfectly one, so that the world may know that thou hast sent me and hast loved them even as thou hast loved me. (John 17: 20–23)

God desires to heal us, giving us the experience of His fullness in community. His union with us isn't complete until we are one with one another. If we perceive God as He is, as Trinity, as community, then our response to Him becomes a response that embodies community. And the characteristics of the relationships within a Christian community are to reflect and participate in the characteristics of the relationships within the Trinity. Community isn't an optional part of God's plan, for those "so inclined" but something at its heart. We need one another for many things, not the least of which is to persevere in personal prayer. And God needs and wants us together not just for our own sakes, but for the sake of the world. God's plan of evangelism is contingent upon there being visible groupings of Christians that show forth by their life together the reality of God's love in their midst, and the true identity of Jesus, our Savior, Savior of the world.

Each Christian is called to community—not to a vague theologically abstract community, but to a flesh-and-blood commitment to a concrete group of people, a commitment expressed in frequent contact, common service and multiple acts of love. Just as God's plan is not for us to be only theoretically in union with Him, with no experience of that union, so His plan is for us not to have just a theoretical, "on paper," union with one another, but one that exists and is expressed in fact.

One of the main ways I had to die to myself in giving my life more fully to God was in renouncing an individualistic way of life to commit myself to other Christians. The early months of this recommitment were painful. I would often have preferred the company of people I found personally attractive to that of the people with whom I shared a bond in Christ. I often would have preferred to be alone, relating with other Christians only when I found it convenient. Ever so gradually, over the years, God has made me increasingly capable of seeing myself as but one of many parts of a body, making decisions and living my life in subordination to the overall good. The commitment to community is not in a separate part of our spiritual life but at its very center.

Although there are some notable exceptions, the average congregation or parish today is far from being a vital Christian community. Relationships among parishioners, even among the most active members, are frequently cold, indifferent, superficial and minimally, if at all, committed. The superficial efforts often employed to "build community," only make the actual reality more painful. Shaking hands at the kiss of peace or at moments of fellowship, however proper in itself, is pathetically short of the commitment to lay down one's life for the brethren that is characteristic of true community. Those expecting the Sunday service alone to build community overlook the fact that many of the worshipers have never made a deep personal commitment to the God they are called to worship. They can scarcely be expected to make such a commitment to one another without a fundamental and serious reorientation of their life and priorities.

God has not abandoned His Church or its local congregations or its individual members. In virtually every country and every congregation, the Spirit of God is stirring to bring the churches back to life. In addition, there are a whole number of prayer and Bible study groups springing up either as offshoots of larger renewal movements or simply as spontaneous developments. A Christian who sees the need for community will be able to find one of these groups close to his home in almost anyplace in the world.[1] Ask the Holy Spirit to lead you to the right one. I cannot recommend any one style of prayer group or any particular movement without knowing each individual situation. Many are very helpful and sound; others have unbalanced leadership and are a menace to authentic renewal. Although I am personally finding valuable community support within the charismatic renewal, I would not want to recommend charismatic prayer groups across the board. I can, however, present some guidelines for finding a group that can provide community support.

· Do the leaders and members have and express a clear commitment to Jesus as Lord and Savior?

· Do the leaders and members have an open and hungry attitude towards the full workings of God's Spirit?

· Do the leaders and members place stress not only on

spiritual experience but on the need to love one another
and develop in Christian character and Christian service,
affirming and living basic Christian morality?

· Do the leaders and members see the group as a leaven to
benefit the wider Christian community of the parish or
church of the members? Do they have positive attitudes
toward and good communication with the priests and ministers of these churches?

✳

There are a number of attitudes that can block our movement toward involvement in Christian community. One of
the most common is expecting a group to be perfect from the
start. After seeing the faults and weaknesses in the members
and leaders of a prayer group or incipient community, many
people decide that they cannot give themselves to such a
thing. This frequently stems from an attitude that considers
oneself better than others. It keeps us from entering the
crucible of patience and suffering in which a community is
often formed. Sometimes this attitude expresses itself in the
attitude that "I'm not getting anything out of the meetings."
But Christian community is not just a matter of receiving,
but of giving. If we are a stronger member of the body, we
should reach out to help our weaker brothers, rather than
withdraw from them in self-satisfaction.

Some people feel they are incapable of community life because of long patterns of individualistic living, or simply a
constitutional aversion. The constitutional aversion is sin,
and the long pattern needs to be changed. Exempting ourselves from community is exempting ourselves from the puri-
fying fire that is the love of God.

Some people experience an initial awkwardness in relating
together—especially in praying together—but this awkward-

ness passes as we get to know each other better and become accustomed to group prayer.

Some people feel they simply do not need community to function as Christians. You may not need it to function on the level you are now functioning, but God wants much more from you and for you. Community is His way.

Sometimes fear holds us back from serious involvement with other Christians. It may be fear that we are not ready to live under the same roof with others or pool all our possessions. That is very seldom what the Lord is calling people to do at the beginning, and it may never be what the Lord wants you to do. Fearing what He may ask, or misunderstanding what He is calling us to, blocks us from what God has for us now.

Another fear is that of becoming unhealthily dependent on other people. God is calling us to a healthy and mature interdependence, not an immature dependency. A community cannot function well unless its members are freely and maturely capable of giving themselves to others. A community cannot function well unless its members are using their gifts and abilities and their maximal human resources, under the Lordship of Jesus, for the common good.

Still another fear is that of losing our personality in the group. Sometimes this fear arises because we sense that we are changing and "losing" something we once had. Perhaps we were once the life of the party, and we find ourselves becoming strangely silent. Or perhaps we were always playing a musical instrument or writing, and we find our interests shifting. Most commonly, this is the reconstruction process of the Holy Spirit, taking us apart and putting us back together again. Life, gifts, talents, customary ways of relating, have almost always been penetrated with self-glorification or rooted in insecurity. As God's Spirit works in us, certain of those things die, some to be reborn in new forms able to function more truly and purely and lovingly. If we persevere, the resurrection does come.

Finally, there is sometimes an irrational or nameless fear we feel about the mere idea of Christian community. When I heard about the charismatic Catholics at Duquesne University in 1966, my reaction was mixed, but it included some simple irrational fear. I think that something in me that was not right sensed its impending death, sensed that the Lord was about to deal with it through contact with the charismatic movement. Since then I have learned that whenever I become irrationally hostile or irritated about some new suggestion connected with Christianity, there is a good chance that a sore spot in need of healing has been touched. I have learned to become more co-operative, recognizing irrational hostility or opposition on my part as a sign that God wants to do something.

I suppose we sense that God will use Christian community to do something major in our lives and are afraid. We must remember that, as with everything else, it is because of His immense love that He wants us to be with Him and with one another.

CHAPTER EIGHT

THE JOY OF ANSWERED PRAYER:
OUR HERITAGE AS SONS

AFTER I returned to Christ and experienced the power of His Spirit in my life I began to feel that I should pray for particular people and situations. Frequently, I would see the things I prayed for happen. Sometimes it was small matters—locked doors opening, lost objects found, guidance given for small decisions. Sometimes it was more serious matters—people being healed, significant financial difficulties resolved, people coming to know the Lord for themselves. Answered prayer has become a regular feature in many people's lives in the restoration of full Christian life God is currently undertaking. Just a few months ago a remarkable series of answered prayers took place in the life of my family and household.

After a year of graduate school in New Jersey, I felt the Lord calling me to a simple life style that would make me more fully available to Him. Since then I have always worked in some sort of Christian service providing only subsistence wages. When I married, my wife shared this approach to service and finances. And for the last three years, we have had other Christians living with us who have also adopted this way of life. During this past summer we felt the Lord wanted us to bring a few more people into our home. We felt that we would need a larger place to live, and began to pray that the

Lord would lead us to a large house that we could rent. We assumed that we would continue to rent since we had no money for a down payment and no credit rating for a mortgage.

At the same time, another family in the community was also expanding their household and needed to find a larger place to live in by the end of August, which was only a few weeks away. We decided to tell them that they could move into our house then, although we might have to share the house for a little while.

No houses appeared for rent, but we heard about a six-bedroom house for sale only a few miles from where we lived. I was in Indiana at the time and my wife told me about the house on the phone. For some reason I felt it might be the place the Lord had for us. When I returned the next day, we all went to take a look: it was perfect for our needs. The only drawback was the cost—$46,900.

As I have said, we had no money for a down payment and no credit rating for a mortgage loan, but we knew the Lord wanted us to have that house. Our realtor, who is also a member of our community, told us of one financial arrangement by which we might be able to buy it. We would not have to obtain a mortgage for several years, by which time we would have enough equity to qualify, but we would need to make a down payment of at least $7,000. We told him to prepare the offer, and asked the Lord to provide the money.

One person in the household did own some stock, but it had been given him by his grandmother, and was earmarked for another purpose. We didn't know if she would allow him to cash the stocks in for our house, but he decided to ask her. She agreed. Then the community managed to scrape together a few thousand dollars and gave it as salary bonuses to four of us who work in community services at subsistence wages. A man in the community donated another large sum from his own pocket. Within a few days we had $7,000 and presented our offer to the owners.

It was rejected. They wanted either a larger down payment, on the order of $10,000 or a full cash payment (which meant a mortgage). By now, the end of August had come, and there were two full households living in our house, in a peace that surprised us all.

The community could not give us any more money, and no one else had any reserves of stocks. Once again, we turned to the Lord, asking him to provide us with $3,000 more.

In another city, friends of ours were also praying for our situation. They asked the Lord if they should give us the money we needed. Opening the Scriptures at random, they saw I Cor. 9:11:

If we have sown spiritual good among you, is it too much
if we reap your material benefits?

I had helped them spiritually; they sent the needed money.

Although we now had the necessary down payment, our chances for getting the house looked worse than ever. Another person, one who could qualify for a mortgage, was interested in it, and had already made a verbal offer. The owners were also having their doubts about selling to a large group like ours: Were we some kind of hippie commune?

We continued to pray and decided to make our second offer despite the obstacles. Unknown to us, two things were happening.

Our realtor went to talk to the owners' lawyer, who was handling the sale. He went simply to tell him that we could make a larger down payment, but in the end spent over an hour with the lawyer, sharing his personal experience of coming to the Lord and telling him about life in a Christian community.

At the same time, one of the owners was talking to a neighbor across the street, telling her their misgivings about the group of people trying to buy the house. She asked the neighbor if she had ever heard of our community. It just so happened that the neighbor was a regular participant in our prayer meetings.

The next day our offer was accepted. The following day we signed the sales agreement. And the day after that we began to move in. It was exactly one week since we had looked at the house for the first time.

This was a remarkable testimony to us of God's love and care and the power of prayer. We had experienced ourselves more deeply than ever before as a "little flock" depending entirely upon the Father for our needs, and seeing His care demonstrated again and again.

God wants to care for us in ways like this. He wants to give us a sense of what to pray for and wants to answer our prayers. Jesus told His disciples time and again that they could ask the Father for things and see them granted, because they too were now His sons. Jesus sounds almost eager for them to try out their privileges as sons.

Truly, truly, I say to you, if you ask anything of the Father, he will give it to you in my name. Hitherto you have asked nothing in my name, ask, and you will receive, that your joy may be full. (Jn. 16:23–24)
If you abide in me, and my words abide in you, ask whatever you will, and it shall be done for you. By this my Father is glorified, that you bear much fruit, and so prove to be my disciples . . . These things I have spoken to you, that my joy may be in you, and that your joy may be full. (Jn. 15:7–11)

And this is the confidence which we have in him that if we ask anything according to his will he hears us. And if we know that he hears us in whatever we ask, we know that we have obtained the requests made of him. (I Jn. 5:14–15)

It is clear that Jesus wants His disciples to have the joy of seeing their prayers answered; that this is an essential part of the salvation He has won for them, and an important characteristic of a full and mature relationship with the Father as sons. God wants His people to know how to ask Him for things so that their joy may be full. Jesus' disciples will lack something if they do not enter into the privileges of sonship He has won for them and learn the secrets of intercessory prayer.

Sometimes young Christians, or old Christians for that matter, focus on promises from the Scripture, like those cited above, and attempt to act on them. When nothing happens, they face a strong temptation to resentment and cynicism about God's love for men. As with all the important topics treated in Scripture, we need to look at the context of Jesus' remarks and the totality of things He says to understand Him correctly. What is the wisdom Jesus gives His disciples about the conditions for effective intercessory prayer?

ABIDING IN HIM

Jesus speaks at length in Chapter 15 of John's gospel about our union with Him, telling us to abide in Him as intimately as branches abide in the vine. He then repeats His promise of answered prayer, explicitly relating it to the necessity of abiding in Him.

If you abide in me, and my words abide in you, ask whatever you will, and it shall be done for you. By this my

Father is glorified; that you bear much fruit, and so prove
to be my disciples. (Jn. 15:7–8)

The relationship implied in the image of the vine and the
branches is obviously quite deep. Jesus adds that His *words*
must abide in us, that what He teaches and reveals and requests must take life in our lives if we are to ask and receive in
prayer. And He makes it clear that God is glorified when men
prove by the fruitfulness of their lives, including their effectiveness in intercessory prayer, that they are truly joined to
Jesus. There is no getting around it: Effectiveness in intercessory prayer is directly related to holiness, our union and con-
formity to the person and teaching of Jesus. These glorious
promises cannot be superficially claimed by those not in such
union with Jesus; to do so is to mock the realities of the relationship involved.

ASKING "IN THE NAME OF JESUS"

It is quite common for people reading the promise of Jesus
quoted earlier in this chapter about asking "in my name" to
conclude every intercessory prayer with the words "in the
name of Jesus," looking to this as a magical formula that en-
sures results. Asking "in the name of Jesus" means asking in
accordance with His most profound and deep intentions and
purposes, asking out of familiarity with them and in harmony with them. A "name" in Scripture denotes an invoca-
tion of a person's whole being, not merely the word that will
get His attention. To be able to ask "in the name of Jesus" is
to ask out of an abiding union and knowledge of Him, and in
accordance with His purposes.

ACCORDING TO HIS WILL

Asking out of an abiding union with Him implicitly means
asking according to His will, asking for something that is in

keeping with the purposes of God. This is specified in Scripture in I Jn. 5:14–15:

> And this is the confidence which we have in him, that if we ask anything according to his will he hears us. And if we know that he hears us in whatever we ask, we know that we have obtained the requests made of him.

Before we ask for something we ought to consider before the Lord whether it is according to His will and purposes or not. This requires familiarity with God's purposes as expressed in Scripture as well as sensitivity to the Holy Spirit's leading as to the time, place, and form in which the desired action of God should take place. When we have reasonable assurance from the Word and the Spirit that something is in accordance with God's will, we can ask with confidence. For example, I know from Scripture it is God's will that all men be saved, so I can pray with confidence for a particular person to come to know the Lord. Unless I receive a special leading from the Lord, however, I cannot with confidence specify the means of the conversion or the time.

The realization that we need to ask with a certain purity of heart, in accordance with God's will and purpose, helps us to understand why so much prayer is not effective. In his epistle, James puts his finger on some of the obvious reasons:

> . . . You do not have, because you do not ask. You ask and do not receive, because you ask wrongly, to spend it on your passions. Unfaithful creatures! Do you not know that friendship with the world is enmity with God? . . . Submit yourselves therefore to God. Resist the devil and he will flee from you. Draw near to God and he will draw near to you. Cleanse your hands, you sinners, and purify your hearts, you men of double mind. . . . Humble

yourselves before the Lord and he will exalt you. (Jas. 4:2–4; 7–10)

ACTING RIGHTLY IN OUR RELATIONSHIPS

In the book of Sirach we are told to honor our parents, so our prayers may not be hindered (Sirach 3:5). In Peter's first letter (3:7) he commends us, "Likewise, you husbands, live considerately with your wives . . . in order that your prayers may not be hindered." And there is Jesus' own warning that if our brother has something against us, or things are not right in our relationships with our brethren, we should go to settle these things before we approach him in prayer. (Mt. 5:23–24.)

Fundamental patterns of injustice or selfishness in our family or business life can also hinder our prayers and must be resolved if God is to grant our requests. In this respect, our contribution or involvement in social justice or injustice affects our relationship with God.

> They seek me day after day,
> they long to know my ways . . .
> they long for God to draw near . . .
> Look you do business on your fastdays,
> you oppress all your workmen;
> look, you quarrel and squabble when you fast
> and strike the poor man with your fist.
> Fasting like yours today
> will never make your voice heard on high. . . .
> Is not this the sort of fast that pleases me . . .
> —it is the Lord Yahweh who speaks—
> to break unjust fetters
> and undo the thongs of the yoke,
> to let the oppressed go free
> and break every yoke,
> to share your bread with the hungry,

and shelter the homeless poor,
to clothe the man you see to be naked
and not turn from your own kin?
Then will your light shine like the dawn
and your wound be quickly healed over . . .
Cry, and Yahweh will answer;
call, and he will say, 'I am here.'
If you do away with the yoke,
the clenched fist, the wicked word,
if you give your bread to the hungry,
and relief to the oppressed,
your light will rise in the darkness,
and your shadows become like noon.
Yahweh will always guide you,
He will give strength to your bones
and you shall be like a watered garden,
like a spring of water
whose waters never run dry. (Isaiah 58:2–11)

In short, sin can hinder prayer.

PRAYING WITH FAITH

In many examples of effective intercessory prayer in the gospels Jesus commends the person who has asked for something for his faith. Let us take a look at several of these incidents and consider what is being said.

In Mark 7:24–30 Jesus is approached by a Gentile woman who falls at His feet and begs Him to cast an evil spirit out of her daughter. He replies, "Let the children first be fed, for it is not right to take the children's bread and throw it to the dogs," indicating that it was not yet time to bring His message to the Gentiles. She persists and answers, "Yes, Lord; yet even the dogs under the table eat the children's crumbs." Jesus responds to her persistence and humility by freeing her daughter.

In Mark 9:21–29 a father brings his son who is gravely afflicted by an evil spirit to Jesus, and asks that Jesus help him ". . . if you can." Jesus replies, "If you can! All things are possible to him who believes." Immediately the father of the child cries out, "I believe, help my unbelief." The boy was freed. The boy's father turns to Jesus with the faith he has, weak and wavering as it is, and that is enough for Jesus to use His power and free the boy.

In Mark 10:13–16 we meet another situation that teaches us about how Jesus wants people to come to Him in faith, directly and simply.

And they were bringing children to him, that he might touch them; and the disciples rebuked them. But when Jesus saw it he was indignant, and said to them, "Let the children come to me, don't hinder them; for to such belongs the kingdom of God. Truly, I say to you, whoever does not receive the kingdom of God like a child shall not enter it." And he took them in his arms and blessed them, laying his hands upon them.

Jesus was *indignant* in this incident. In the previous one He was disturbed at someone doubting His power. He is making painfully clear how much He wants us to trust in His power, to trust in His immense love and goodness that wants to receive us and our requests.

In Mark 10:46–52 we read of Bartimaeus who did not care what people thought of him, or what social convention or social pressure had to be gone against to get to Jesus and make contact with Him. Bartimaeus was a blind beggar who was sitting by the roadside as Jesus passed. He began to cry out, "Jesus, Son of David, have mercy on me!" And many rebuked him telling him to be silent; but he cried out all the more. "Son of David have mercy on me!" And Jesus stopped and said, "Call him" . . . and throwing off his mantle he sprang up and came to Jesus. And Jesus said to him, "What do you want me to do for you?" And the blind man said to Him, "Master let me receive my sight." And Jesus said to him, "Go your way; your faith has made you well." And immediately he received his sight and followed Him on the way.

In all the incidents Jesus blesses those who in their need turn to Him with their whole hearts, who are not held back by what people think, and who arc not ashamed to let their need show. Their deepest human emotions are involved—a mother seeking desperately for a cure for her daughter, a father for his son, a blind man for his sight. We see single-mindedness and determination; we see persistence through obstacles, whether the apparent response of God Himself (the Gentile woman) or the social pressure of "friends" (Bartimaeus). We see Jesus responding with equal depth of emotion, reaching out to the depth of the human need that turns to Him for its solution. We see Him pointedly, almost desperately, insisting on receiving the people who come to Him with such naturalness and honesty of need and faith, indignant at those who would hinder or block them.

Many of us in the Church today have had our life with God and our approach to Him atrophied. It has often become an intellectual, religiously correct, theologically contained, partial response or approach or request. The Jesus we see in the gospels reaches out to real people who are not ashamed to let their need be expressed, not afraid to abandon their pride, their cool, their social standing, their "position" to kneel before Him and speak the awful burden of their hearts, the agony that tears them apart. As persons they came to Him: with head, heart, spirit, body. That is the kind of approach to God we very much need today. We need to rediscover ourselves as full human beings and discover that it is precisely as full human beings that God wants us to come to Him. His salvation, His love, His mercy is designed for full human beings, not theological or religious creatures who have stifled their humanity or repressed their deepest emotions.

If I could sum up in one word the quality of faith I see in the Gospels, it would be to call it a "gutsy" faith, a faith that is full-bodied and alive with the direct call of "deep calling to deep." It is persistent, it is aggressive, it is direct, it is simple, it is imperfect, it is hungry, it is earnest—but it is real. We ought to be fully human and unashamed of our humanity, our concern for our daughter or son, for our own sight, as we approach the God who made us that way and is waiting for us to come to Him in that way.

Jesus Himself approached God in that way and communicated with His whole heart in prayer to the Father.

For we have not a high priest who is unable to sympathize with our weaknesses, but one who in every respect has been tempted as we are, yet without sinning. Let us then with confidence draw near the throne of grace that we may receive mercy and find grace to help in time of need. . . . In the days of his flesh, Jesus offered up prayers and supplications with loud cries and tears, to him who was able to save him from death, and he was heard for his godly fear. (Heb. 4:15–16; 5:7)

The Spirit is imparting to our heart the faith and desire to approach God.

PRAYER WITH FASTING

Prayer with fasting was a regular part of the New Testament Church. Jesus Himself recommended it for particularly difficult prayer needs, and we see the early Church practicing it for particular needs. For example, in Acts 13:2–3 and 14: 23, prayer and fasting accompanies the sending out of Barnabas and Saul, and the choosing of a group of elders. In my own life and the life of our community, I have seen the Lord use prayer and fasting as a way of turning us more deeply and earnestly to Himself in intercession.

Shortly after I gave my life back to the Lord I felt that I should take a special responsibility for praying for my family, and felt that it should be done with some moderate fasting. I took every Tuesday to specially remember my family in prayer accompanied by fasting, skipping a meal or something like that. This continued for a number of years (often the Lord wants us to persist in prayer; e.g., Lk. 11:5–10) and gradually I saw the Lord bring, at different times, three of my sisters to an explicit recommitment of their lives to Him, saw them receive a release of the Holy Spirit, and saw two of them led to deeply committed Christian husbands. All three now live in Christian communities and are actively involved in serving the Lord. My parents, younger brother and other sister, are gradually being brought to the same renewal of Christian life and have come from positive hostility to what was happening to us to being very supportive and open.

Just this past year I felt on several occasions that the Lord was calling those living in our house to a special day of prayer and fasting for a particular person. Each time we saw the Lord work in strong and definite ways in response.

Fasting is not supposed to be a burden; it is given as an additional means to intensify the turning of our hearts to God and to increase the earnestness of our prayer.

✳

Do not get discouraged by where you are as regards abiding with the Lord. There is an important, essential link between holiness and regularly fruitful intercession, but God is willing to start with us where we are. Start praying for what seems within reach of your faith and union, even if the things are simple and small. Some of my most joyful moments still come when Jesus starts the car on freezing winter days, or finds the key that has been lost, or stops a cold that was sure to develop into something more.

Also, rather than using a scattergun approach and praying for everything under the sun all the time, pick out a few things to pray regularly for, and expect to see results. Consider before the Lord what one or two or three specific needs or people He wants you to pray for and make this a regular daily practice, looking for the results. Be specific in the requests, after forming the request in prayer, and be persistent. When things don't seem to be working out, ask the Lord for understanding why. There are still many unexplained prayer mysteries in my own life, but the Holy Spirit, despite what I don't understand about why a particular situation didn't seem to work out, seems to be ever renewing my desire to pray again. Don't be afraid to make mistakes. Expect to. Expect the Holy Spirit to teach you more and more about intercessory prayer. It's your heritage as sons and daughters of God.

CHAPTER NINE

GOING ON WITH GOD

A FRIEND OF MINE asked Kathryn Kuhlman to autograph the flyleaf of her book *I Believe in Miracles* for him. The words she wrote were: "To Al, there's *more*, there's *so much more*. Kathryn." There is always more, so much more, that God wants us to know of His love.

I'd like to share an experience I had last year that the Lord used to reveal more of His Love. I was in Rome for the first international leaders conference of the Catholic charismatic renewal. This was the conference where the Pope received a small group of us in a private audience and spoke his first words of public encouragement concerning the good fruit coming from the charismatic renewal.[1] On our first night there one of the Jesuit priests who had come for the conference invited a few of us to go with him to visit the house where Ignatius of Loyola had lived and died. Ignatius, the founder of the order to which he belonged, had lived and worked in the sixteenth century and had been instrumental in helping many people find a deeper life in Christ.

I went with him, not knowing what to expect, since the whole cult of the saints of the Catholic Church had become a background part of my life. I really didn't know quite how to make sense of it in light of the need for the overwhelming centrality of Christ to stand out clearly. Also, I was concerned about the unfortunate practical results of exalting a few great Christians, "the saints," in a way that gave people the idea that full union with God was only for the few and not for the whole people of God, for "the saints" in the broader, New Testament meaning of the word. A few months previously, in fact, I had visited a prominent Catholic cathedral dedicated to St. Joseph in another country, and it sure seemed that someone going through the cathedral could easily get the impression that St. Joseph was a Savior, and the one to whom people in need ought to turn, in a way that all but obscured the unique role of Jesus as Savior and Lord.

As we arrived at the section of the building where St. Ignatius lived something began to happen within me. I began to experience the presence of God in a marked way, and I began to feel my heart drawn to a single-minded love for Jesus. As we walked into the room where he slept and worked, and where he prayed and celebrated the Lord's Supper, the sense of God's presence deepened. I felt as though the Holy Spirit was showing me that the important thing about Ignatius for me to know was how much he loved Jesus and how single-mindedly he dedicated his life to drawing men to a deep dedication to Jesus, and how deeply Jesus lived within him. I also began to experience Ignatius present *with us*, in what God was doing today in bringing about a true gospel renewal of His people, in a way that was encouraging and inspiring, in a way that moved me to a deeper love for Jesus and a desire to serve Him more completely, as Ignatius himself had done in his day.

Ignatius is with Jesus now and with us, as an elder brother in the Lord who by his life and example and active concern for us now is moving us on to love of Jesus. It began to click what the "cult of the saints and Mary" could mean. I saw

their transparency and how when we truly came into contact with them, we noticed not so much them, but Jesus
within them, and found our hearts and attention turning, not
so much to them as to the One who dwells within them, the
One whom they serve.

Something of the same thing happened the next day as we
drove to Assisi on the eve of the conference to pray for the
outpouring of God's Spirit upon it. I could see there—even
through what the town had done to capitalize on the fact that
St. Francis had lived and died there, and what cultural Catholicism had done to put Francis in the center rather than
Jesus—another example of a man who had burned with love
for Jesus and had given his life and heart to him in a totally
abandoned way. In Assisi where I experienced God's presence
most was not at Francis' tomb—which spoke of the earthly
remains of Francis in rather too central a way for me—but
rather in the ruins of his father's house and the place where
his own room was, even though it had been overlaid with
marble, and the little church called San Damiano which he
had helped rebuild with his own hands, and the place where
he and Clare and the other early followers of Jesus at that
time prayed and talked and sought God. It was while standing in his room that I felt moved to kneel, in the presence
of God, and recall how he had struggled here to come to grips
with the mystery of God's love and call and had decided to
follow Him with his whole life. I experienced the presence of
Francis with us too, as a quiet encouragement to what God
was doing today, and how, yes, Jesus was calling me and all
of us on to that single-minded love for Jesus that Francis
himself had. Meeting Francis I had come to meet Jesus and
see what it was to respond to Him in a new way.

The second night of the conference Cardinal Suenens was
celebrating the Eucharist and I was sitting near the back,

resting from some of my conference responsibilities. In the midst of my tiredness I felt the Spirit opening up a deeper level of my being to the love of God, and in the midst of tears, turned to God in a fuller way than ever and told Him I wanted always to be with Him and follow Him as Ignatius and Francis had. And I felt that the Spirit was freeing me in a new way to follow the Lord more fully, and experience His love more deeply.

As we're faithful to the Lord in our daily lives, there come moments like this, when what the Holy Spirit has been preparing in us "beneath the surface" becomes manifest and blossoms into a new stage. And it's this inner, transforming action of the Spirit that I'd like to talk about in these concluding pages.

✣

We have talked about many major components for union with God in prayer. Many of these are objective and definite actions that produce definite results, such as accepting Christ fully as our Lord and Savior, asking to be baptized in the Spirit, taking concrete steps to have contact with other committed Christians seeking a deeper life in the Spirit in community, setting aside a time each day for personal prayer. The importance of these definite acts cannot be underestimated. On the other hand, as important as the objective actions are, they are intended only to make us more accessible to the true goal of our life—union with God, the full maturity of the seed of new life. This book has tried to present the elements of the foundation we need to allow the Holy Spirit to effectively have access to us and work in us. If the way of prayer is followed, it will accomplish God's full purpose. I would like to end by giving some images or models, of the dynamics of the working of the Spirit within us as we follow the way of prayer, and some suggestions that may help us more fully yield to His workings and to God's final goal.

The dynamics of inner transformation can be looked at profitably under many different aspects. One way of looking at what the Holy Spirit does within us as we persevere in prayer is that He brings our mind, heart and will into communion with the mind, heart and will of Christ. In Romans 12:2 Paul talks about having our minds renewed by the Spirit rather than being conformed to the thinking of the world.

Our minds have been formed in their thinking by many forces and factors opposed to Christ. We can compare, for example, the way we think of material and bodily security and the way Jesus Himself looks at those things (Lk. 12:22–34). He invites us to join Him in his way of thinking, based on the truth of our Father's care for us. We can be as free as Jesus regarding food and clothing. We can live first for the kingdom of God.

Our emotions too have been formed by many influences. Many of us are ruled in our approach to people by deep-rooted fear or suspicion, or by anger or resentment. We can literally be enslaved—kept from freedom—by our emotions. As we grow in union with God, those emotions are laid bare and the light of the Holy Spirit begins to free us and heal us from being slaves to them. At the same time He begins to impart to us a participation in what I think one can call the "emotions" of God Himself. We begin to feel more and more as God "feels" about people and things, participating in the compassion, love, anguish, anger, restraint and determination of Jesus Himself. As they grow in union with Him everyone will begin to have their emotions function in union with the emotions of Christ. Reading the Gospels with an eye to understanding the feelings of Christ in different situations can be a real help in freeing our own emotions to work properly and constructively.

Love, as experienced in the most intense of human relationships between husband and wife, parent and child, is frequently the vehicle God uses to manifest His similar love. He invites me to participate more fully with Him in His love, as He participates more fully with me in my love as father and husband. This is God's way of revealing Himself in the very midst of our life, in the heart of our relationships. There are occasions and circumstances for all of us, married or single, to discover and participate in it in a fuller way.

Our wills too need to be transformed. Even when we have committed our lives to God, many of us have been surprised a year or five years later to discover how deeply our self-will is still operative. In fundamental and important ways we can relate to Christ, to other people, to the Christian community and to life itself *on our own terms*. God then brings us to a point of crisis where our self-will is directly confronted and forced to make a decision more deeply than ever before, to submit or to rebel. Sometimes this deeper revelation of our own self-will and the extent to which it has controlled even our Christian life is enough to produce for the most dedicated Christian a genuine crisis of faith, in which the pain of deep submission is such that whether to go on with the Lord or not actually comes into question. When submission at this deep level takes place, self-will truly can be "broken" and a new level of relating to the Lord and submitting to the movings of His Spirit can be reached. It can be a shock to discover that we are praying or serving other people just up to the point where it pleases us or suits our image of ourself. For some this happens suddenly in intense crises; for others it happens gradually, almost imperceptibly over a period of years. God has His way of working with each of us, but it is the same work He is about and it certainly involves a "breaking" of self-will so that God's will can save and give life.

God is freeing us to participate more and more consciously with Him and Jesus and the Spirit in Their life of love and commitment and union. That is what Jesus promised, and that is what His Spirit is working to produce. His Spirit is mingled with our spirit. He is side by side with us, as an older brother with a younger brother, helping, encouraging, prodding, pulling, nurturing, leading. His Spirit is in *intimate* contact with our spirit and is actively influencing, gently working to heal us and free us and help us to see, most of all preparing us to see what, or rather who we have received— *Jesus and the Father within us.* Growing in prayer is letting Jesus and the Father more and more fully live within us and work through us, flowing from the depths of our being, forming us to be a manifestation, instrument, participator in Their divine life and mission.

✳

God calls us on. He will transform us. To give Him full freedom, we must do our part in removing the obstacles to His action in our lives. The obstacle that I'd like to consider now is that of fear, for it is often at the root of many of our resistances to God.

One of the things that holds many of us back from more fully yielding ourselves to God is the fear that we are not going to be able to live up to it, or carry through with that kind of commitment. Well, we are not if we look at it as being a matter of our own strength, our own fidelity, our own perseverance. But that is to look at life with Christ as an obstacle course or a law or a burden. He wants to give a gift, and we need to let go to receive it. The more we let go the more He can give. The gift is Himself, His Holy Spirit, which now from within us strengthens our weakness and provides "power from on high" to enable us to live the Christian life. Awareness of our inadequacy and weakness can hold us back from commitment and cause despair and discouragement, or it can be an occasion for making a commitment, knowing we cannot carry it out on our own strength, and having literally and actually to depend on the power of God to carry it out.

This is precisely the point at which authentic Christianity begins; when we know our own weaknesses and inadequacies and know we cannot live that kind of life on our own strength. If we could live it on our own strength, we would not have needed a Savior, and would not have needed Pentecost. Sometimes it is pride that makes us want to wait until we can do things without making a mistake, holding back from committing ourselves to ensure that we will "look good" and not be a "failure." We need to know we are a failure at holiness in order to become holy, in order to qualify for "divine welfare." We need to admit our incapacity for following the Lord faithfully so that He can begin to take over within us. Becoming aware of our inadequacies and weaknesses puts us in a position where God's power can be manifest within us.

And to keep me from being too elated by the abundance of revelations, a thorn was given me in the flesh, a messenger of Satan, to harass me, to keep me from being too elated. Three times I besought the Lord about this, that it should leave me; but he said to me, "My grace is sufficient for you, for my power is made perfect in weakness." I will all the more gladly boast of my weaknesses, that the power of Christ may rest upon me. For the sake of Christ, then, I am content with weaknesses, insults, hardships, persecutions, and calamities; for when I am weak, then I am strong. (II Cor. 12:7–10)

Christianity is not saving ourselves, but being saved by Christ. We are not supposed to earn our salvation through our

efforts but accept it as a gift from the Lord. Receiving it from
Him releases a power within us that enables us to live out the
commitment.

> For by grace you have been saved through faith; and this
> is not your own doing, it is the gift of God—not because
> of works, lest any man should boast. (Eph. 2:8–9)

Make the commitment, put your faith in Him for the power
to carry it out.

Sometimes this fear of failure and feeling of inadequacy is
fed by the way spiritual renewal movements take shape and
express themselves. It is common for the more dramatic conversion stories to become predominant, and the more articulate among us and the ones with the most out-going personalities and most vivid experiences to dominate the sharing.
This can sometimes cause people to feel like they're in a different world, that nothing is happening to them, that they
can't experience God like that. Several other things are factors
also. One is that different temperaments respond differently
to the Lord. Some temperaments are seemingly more open
to immediate and strong experiences. Others come to an
awareness of God's presence and experience of Him rather
gradually. The former sometimes have more difficulty per-
severing.

Remember the story of the tortoise and the hare. There
are a lot of hares today, and praise God for them, scooting all
around with their spiritual experience, and it is genuine in
most cases, making the tortoises wonder if they're worth anything or capable of being Christians. In the story it was
through steady faithfulness and plodding along that the
tortoise ended up winning the race. Hopefully heaven will be
full of vast quantities of tortoises and hares, but it is important for people of more quiet temperaments not to feel con-

demned by the more lively among us, and to steadfastly move on with the Lord in daily fidelity.

Another reason, though, for the feelings of condemnation that Satan takes advantage of is loose "God talk." A jargon can develop in spiritual renewal movements, in which God is genuinely acting, that can give a misleading picture of the precise thing that's being experienced. Hearing people talk in terms of "God told me this, and God told me that, and then I said to Him and then He said to me," etc., can give a very misleading picture of what's actually happening. People who don't easily use the language or know it can begin to feel like they're in a different spiritual world even when they're not. When that talk is being used, often what is meant is, "I sensed God telling me, or I felt like He was showing me something, or it seemed to me from the Lord" or whatever. Usually it's not an audible voice, or even an interior sensation as is experienced in prophecy, but more a sense or a feeling, that indeed can be from the Lord, but not with the directness and immediacy and form in which it is loosely expressed.

Sometimes too it is just a matter of consciousness. Sometimes God is acting and leading and teaching and doing things in people's lives and they're just not used to noticing those things or attributing them to the Lord. Some people are very conscious of what God is doing and are used to talking about it. Some people are remarkably unconscious and not used to talking about it, but often are having it happen to them without them being fully aware. I've sat in sharing groups where someone very articulately talked at length about God acting in his life in fairly ordinary ways and made it sound extraordinary. Other people in the group have said they had nothing to share and were not aware of what God was doing in their lives, or didn't think He was doing anything, when I knew them very well and knew that God was doing a lot.

Asking the Holy Spirit to make us more aware of what God is doing and more sensitive to it is a help in supporting spiritual growth.

Another fear stems from our vision of the distance between God and man. Sin has tragically and dramatically separated us from the awareness and fulfillment that remains the base of our relationship with God. For a long time it was a puzzle to me how God and man could have anything to do with one another. What does Spirit have to do with flesh? What can they have to do with one another? How could one ever feel at home with the other? The Holy Spirit has helped me to understand and experience the primordial union that existed between God and man, and the way we are formed in the depths of our being to be in union with Him. The resistances, the distances, the sense of dissimilarity is the disfigurement that marred the original creation—it is not the most basic truth about ourselves and God.

Originally, pure Spirit and flesh existed together in harmony and union. After the profound rupture of that union through man's rebellion, God became committed not just to restoring the original union, but even to going beyond it. The Word of God, the second person of the Godhead, originally pure Spirit like the Father and Holy Spirit, expressed the commitment of God to the human race by eternally joining Himself to the lot of men, in flesh and blood, in the incarnation of Jesus. God has eternally joined Himself to flesh and blood. Dwelling among us, undergoing the human condition experiencing the deep evil that plagues and afflicts human life, emptying Himself out to the uttermost, to the point of death, rising victorious, now still flesh and blood, and eternally flesh and blood, eternally human, He stands radiant and transfigured, His human body reconstituted in the resurrection.

He offers the same resurrection, transfiguration and eternal life to all who come to Him.

God invites us into the profound unity of the trinity, "making us partake of the divine nature!" The degree to which God seeks to enfold man and embrace man and heal man and raise man up and take man to His bosom is deep beyond words. One becomes silent as the Holy Spirit reveals to us the love of God expressed in the life, death, and resurrection of Jesus.

Another of the most common fears keeping us from giving our lives fully to God is the fear of sacrifice. There is no question but that Jesus says some hard sayings and that the saving message is "strong medicine." If they were softened, they would no longer be strong enough medicine to deal with the sickness in our lives. There is a letting go, a death to self involved. The pain, the death, the sacrifice is not an end in itself, it is to produce new life, to deal with what in us is distorting our personality and relationships, and free us from the bonds that keep us from experiencing the glorious freedom of the sons of God, from knowing Him and the power of His resurrection. Knowing what lies beyond the letting go—the receiving of the Holy Spirit in greater and greater measure, being healed, set free, liberated—makes it possible to bear the pain gladly, in joy. When we hold onto things and seek to save and control them ourselves, they fall apart in our hands. When we let go of them and give them to God to order, they take on a new radiance, and bring a new peace and joy to our lives. Many things we give up to God are returned sooner or later with a new loveliness to them, although there is no denying that when we give things up God indeed may not return them to us in that form at all.

For me, giving my life over to Christ meant giving up a career, a relationship, a set of friends and a way of life that were not right, a style of operating that was exciting but sinful. It meant giving up the way I spent my time, and the right to decide for myself how to spend it. It meant giving up the writing and editorial work I had been involved in. It meant making Christ the most important person in my life, and subordinating all else to Him. It meant submitting myself in obedience to the Christian community, and in a special way to those I lived and worked with. It meant a crucifixion of self-will that has produced major changes in my character, and is still producing them. It was three years before I was ready to consider marriage. It was over five years before I was able to use the writing and editorial gifts the Lord had given me in a way that would bring glory to Him and life to men. Some of what I have given up to the Lord has been returned; some of it has not, but my life has deepened in Him and I praise Him for all He has done.

Another common fear that keeps us from God is rooted in the belief that "I've made a fatal wrong turning, a basic mistake, and now it's all over, there's no hope of living a deep life of union with God." Whether it be a suggestion to the effect that you should never have dropped out of school, or you married the wrong person, or you never should have married, or you never should have chosen celibacy, or you never should have had nine kids, or you never should have left a certain city where there was a Christian community, or whatever; Satan can make use of doubts and suggestions like this to cut us off from God. "The grass is always greener" syndrome is an insidious weapon that Satan uses and one that we are vulnerable to. We are where we are, and God is there with us ready to work with us where we are; we may never know how to evaluate some past decisions; if there's something to repent of, repent; if you're not sure after a reasonable time of openness to the Lord or consultation with a mature Christian, forget about it and go on. No mistake or sin, real or imagined, can't be dealt with; God wants to take care of it and wants us to move on with Him from where we are now.

Another block can be fear of God Himself. Our conception of God can be based on a whole number of negative experiences in our families, in our schools, among our friends, in the Church and by chance. Fears of being exploited, of not being loved, or of being used commonly block the free giving of ourselves to God. Because of a negative series of personal relationships in college while I was away from the Lord, I had developed a deep-rooted, almost unconscious, fear of God and other people that blocked receiving their love. Gradually I became aware of the fear, and came to understand its roots in those relationships. Gradually, at first intellectually and then emotionally, I realized there was a difference between the love I had experienced then and the love of God. God's love is pure, holy, gentle, wise, non-exploitive, non-violative. He can be totally trusted. Now I rejoice in receiving God's love in the infinite number of ways in which it is communicated every day, and rejoice to abandon myself to Him, trusting Him completely.

One of the biggest obstacles to abandoning ourselves to God is the fear of not being accepted, not being chosen, not being worthy. We commonly feel that real union with God is for others who are "better" than ourselves and that we are too sinful, too ordinary, too busy, too normal, too messed up or whatever to be close to God. God wants all men to be intimately and tenderly united to Himself. The call to love God with our whole heart, whole soul, whole mind and strength is addressed to all men. What God calls a man to, He gives the means to achieve. God stands ready to meet us where we are, and gradually and gently, step by step, lead us to intimate union with Himself. One of the most damaging lies of Satan is that we have a unique problem or character flaw that makes us incapable of being closely united to God. That ought to be called by its rightful name whenever it surfaces and attempts to do its ugly work of keeping God's people from Himself. You *are* called, you *are* chosen, you *are* able, to be with Him. Anything else is a lie, and its intent is your death, your distance from the God of life, mercy and love.

❖

When we have laid the foundation and dealt with the major obstacles to a deepening union with God in our lives, we can expect to see it happen. We will see God making progress in us. Approaching the question of progress in union with God, however, is a delicate matter. We ought to grow in our knowledge of God and be more fully joined to Him, but self-consciousness and a focus on progress can be the most deadly thing for true union and freedom to happen.

One of the sicknesses in the churches today is the incredible vagueness that exists when it comes to talking about the spiritual life. When "old styles and systems" of spirituality were thrown out, in many cases the baby was thrown out with the bath water. Today's "return to spirituality" is often so vague and muddled that it is impossible to judge whether spiritual progress can be assessed in any way. But it has always been the case, starting with the New Testament and continuing through Christian tradition, that spiritual progress can be evaluated and ought to be happening.

Measuring spiritual progress is not a hopelessly vague, subjective matter; there are quite objective and universally accepting criteria in vital Christianity for evaluating spiritual progress, although there is great danger in applying objective criteria for spiritual progress rigidly or insensitively. Despite all these difficulties, we can say there ought to be progress, and that if there is none, something is wrong.

I'd like to present some objective indicators of growth in union with God. Taken in isolation they may mean nothing. When they form a pattern, over a period of time they can reveal a significant pattern of growth or lack of growth.

· Is serious sin clearing up in the person's life?

· Is intentional less-serious sin clearing up?

· Is the person using more of his time, talent and money in the service of the Lord?

· Is the time spent in prayer being authenticated by a growth in loving behavior with his brethren and loving service to his neighbor?

· Are the fruits of the Holy Spirit (love, joy, peace, patience, gentleness, self-control, etc.) becoming apparent in the person's life, and the works of the flesh (envy, jealousy, lust, quarreling, etc.) receding?

· Is the person willing readily to admit mistakes, to admit wrongdoing, to accept the criticism of others?

Knowing how properly to use these indicators (and others like them) is another matter. It is not uncommon for someone who has rigidly adhered to Christian morality and outwardly charitable behavior to experience *less* self-control, patience, etc. after a real conversion than before. The externally imposed controls are breaking up as the Holy Spirit brings to birth a new set of controls. What appeared to be virtue and Christian character was perhaps a response in fear with no inner transformation. The breakdown of what appeared to be virtue may be an essential part of moving to a better state, and not a sign of lack of progress.

Also great harm can be done if the indicators are applied as weapons to beat somebody over the head. An example: "See, you pray every day, but you still lose your temper. What a phony." Authentic development can be going on internally but hasn't manifested itself yet in the area that might be most visibly deficient. Demanding change in certain areas as a sign of authentic development can be brutally misused. Sensitivity to God's timing and God's plan of development for a person is essential. God may not be intending to reach a certain area until a number of other things get worked out, and forcing the area may be positively harmful. It's something like demanding "social action" from a group of Christians barely at the first stages of loving one another.

Just because there are obvious misuses of these indicators does not mean that they are not helpful in the hands of someone experienced and sensitive to the workings of the Spirit in peoples' lives or in providing an individual with a general framework and vision by which to gauge the soundness of the development of his life. All genuine sources of guidance and help have their practical problems. Nevertheless, they are all we have.

Traditionally, Christians have had good and holy men to turn to who could offer their wisdom and direction in growing in union with God. The major problem today is that there are very few people able to so function, and they are often overburdened. The most promising, practical sources of help today are the prayer groups and communities now developing with an explicit dedication to a revitalized Christian life. The group itself can provide a steady source of encouragement, wisdom and balance, even when its resources in terms of exceptionally gifted people with pastoral and theological training are limited.

Obviously, aberrations can and do happen in such groups. But they happen equally if not more often with all sources of guidance. Obviously, even with group support, there will be limits on what can happen—serious difficulties may not get

cleared up, people may get well-meaning advice that is wrong
—but truly effective and practical guidance and support can
usually be found and progress made. In all this, we need to
remember that God has promised not to leave us orphans.
He Himself is with us to help and guide us through His Holy
Spirit, as well as through the circumstances of our lives.

*

Holy, holy, holy, Lord God of power and might; heaven
and earth are full of your glory, hosanna in the highest;
blessed is he who comes in the name of the Lord, hosanna
in the highest.

"Heaven and earth are filled with the glory of God." God
is everywhere, as our first catechism said. God is everywhere,
always. Prayer is communion with God. It is possible, desirable to commune with God, everywhere and always. When
Paul invites us to pray constantly it is but a logical implica-
tion of the fact that God is everywhere all the time; that
there is no place and no time in which God is not present,
and in which we can't commune with Him. He literally fills
the universe and permeates all that is. Matter itself, the very
creation, reveals Him.

However, we can't always and everywhere become sensitive
to His personal presence unless we are turning to Him in the
concrete, definite, limited ways, that are the keys to opening
us up to His unlimited personal presence. Putting our trust in
Christ, being baptized in the Spirit, becoming part of a vital
Christian community, being faithful in a regular time of personal prayer, all prepare us and free us for experiencing and
partaking in communion with God more and more fully in
all our life. Our life and work don't become a prayer, an act of
communication and love with God, by decreeing it such but
by a gradual process of interior freedom by which our heart
is able more and more to "see" and "sense" God everywhere

and in everything. There are those who try to leap to constant prayer without crawling and walking, and it doesn't work. Yet for those who are following in the way of daily personal prayer, praying always becomes more and more a possibility, a reality.

The name given to Jesus at one point in the Scripture is beautiful: Emmanuel, which means God with us. Jesus promises us that we are not being left orphans but He will be with us always, and His Spirit, and if we love Him and keep His words to us, His Father also. How expressive of this abiding presence of God is the psalm:

> Yahweh, you examine me and know me,
> you know if I am standing or sitting,
> you read my thoughts from far away,
> whether I walk or lie down, you are watching,
> you know every detail of my conduct.
>
> The word is not even on my tongue,
> Yahweh, before you know all about it;
> close behind and close in front you fence me round,
> shielding me with your hand.
> Such knowledge is beyond my understanding,
> a height to which my mind cannot attain.
>
> Where could I go to escape your spirit?
> Where could I flee from your presence?
> If I climb the heavens, you are there,
> there too, if I lie in Sheol.
>
> If I flew to the point of sunrise,
> or westward across the sea,
> your hand would still be guiding me,
> your right hand holding me.
>
> If I asked darkness to cover me,
> and light to become night around me,

that darkness would not be dark to you,
night would be as light as day.

It was you who created my inmost self,
and put me together in my mother's womb;
for all these mysteries I thank you:
for the wonder of myself, for the wonder of your works.

You know me through and through,
from having watched my bones take shape
when I was being formed in secret,
knitted together in the limbo of the womb.

 you had scrutinized my every action,
 all were recorded in your book,
 my days listed and determined,
 even before the first of them occurred.

God, how hard it is to grasp your thoughts!
How impossible to count them!
I could no more count them than I could the sand,
and suppose I could, you would still be with me.

(Ps. 139:1–18)
The Jerusalem Bible

We are distinct beings; we have our own minds, hearts, wills, bodies. Living the spiritual life is not becoming different than we are but allowing God to be with us in what we are, and becoming His in the process. This means changes, but maintaining our distinct identity, and continuing to live within the order of the created, the material. The Trinity is dwelling deep within us. So too is God with His creation. Food, rain, the sun, bread, flowers, cloth, rock, wood, steel, buildings, cars, electricity all have their real identity and autonomy and aren't changed into pure spirit when in right relationship to God. But God is with those things too, intimately. A Russian Orthodox theologian made the statement

at one time: "Food is the divine love made edible." This
expresses something of the reality of God's presence in things.
When we eat, we are indeed eating food. But also, God is
actively, directly loving us in giving us that food—not just in
originating it through creating seeds and setting the wheels
in motion, but He accompanies that food with His love and
presence. He comes to us, truly, in the food, in the sun, in the
clothing we wear, the water we drink, the people who touch
us with love; He accompanies them and comes to us in them.
We can truly receive the Holy Spirit when we receive the
breath of the day into us or the light of the sun or the food
of tonight's supper. We can receive the love of God into us,
God Himself as He accompanies the gifts He gives in His
creation.

Everything, then, tells of Him. He comes to us in everything. Receive Him. When I walk down the street on a sunny
day and look up and glance at the sun I receive its light and
heat and bless the Son of God. When I drink a glass of water,
I appreciate the water and receive the Holy Spirit. One order
of reality, the material, isn't diminished or falsely spiritual-
ized, by being aware of the closeness of another order to it; it
is authentically and properly enriched. God is with us. We
can receive the Holy Spirit not just in the sacraments, not
just in the Eucharist—although those are certainly special
focal points where He communicates Himself especially—not
only in personal prayer time, but in every breath we take,
every ray of sun that hits us, every bite of food we eat, every
drink of water we take, every embrace we receive, every kiss
that is given; God is imparting Himself, bestowing Himself,
pouring Himself out everywhere, always. Receive Him, receive Him. Receive Him now, in the words you read. Receive
Him now as you touch the chair you sit in. Receive Him now

as you look out the window and see the sky, touch the ground, feel a tree, breathe the air.

※

It can be helpful in becoming more aware of God's presence everywhere and always to take advantage of different opportunities during the day outside of our regular prayer time to pause for a few moments and explicitly turn to Him in praise, or in silence, or in petition. Whenever we have a few spare moments between duties, appointments, before typing the next letter, seeing the next patient, changing the next diaper, loading the next load, rather than filling it up with something else, just pause for a few moments, sit down, be quiet and be aware of Him, who is with us always. There are usually several opportunities like this for all of us every day. Taking advantage of them as moments of being aware of Him can make a great difference in our abiding union with Him. Singing while walking down the street or driving in the car or praying or being silent are all ways in which God can come to us and be present to us.

Praying should never be a burden, but a gift. For it to be that it needs to be done in response to the prompting of the Holy Spirit who gives us the desire, helps us hear the call of God, and makes us able to be aware of Him and pray. We, in our weakness, don't know how to pray always, but God's Spirit will help us. Don't strain, don't force anything; if you're not aware of God in drinking a glass of water, fine; sometimes it's fine just to perceive one order of reality and not the other. All will come in due time, if we're faithful to what the Holy Spirit is prompting us to do today.

One of the great snares by which many are kept from God is daydreaming about what they would do if the circumstances were different, or in the future, or in some other responsibility than the one they have now. When Jesus said that

he who is faithful in small things will be put over greater
things He was giving us a guide not just for financial steward-
ship, but for everything pertaining to life with Him (Lk.
16:10). If we are faithful in the duties and responsibilities
and circumstances of today, no matter what they are, and
look to be performing a good job at what we've been entrusted
with today, we can be sure to be in the right place when God
wants to entrust other things to us. Maybe you are being
called to a great ministry in the future, or maybe you are
called to be a wife someday, or maybe you are called to develop your musical talents which you can't do at the moment
because you work as a carpenter. Effective Christian service
flows from Christian character. Christian character is developed through bearing trials patiently and faithfully responding to the grace and responsibilities of today. We will not be
able to sustain a great ministry, the responsibility of being a
wife or of being a musician who communicates the life of
God, unless our innermost man is being strengthened, puri-
fied, broken, made docile to the work of God's Spirit. Saving
our "best" for the future or holding back from putting our
whole hearts into something for today is the surest way of
holding back from God's action in our life. Moses was in a
hidden life for forty years before being ready to lead the
children of Israel. Jesus lived in the life style of a carpenter
for thirty; He learned obedience through suffering. Should we
expect any less? Doing the humblest chore in the right spirit
and with the right attitude can do more to free us for the
work of God within than the most "spiritual, important"
chore done for self-glory or to satisfy "needs" of our own. In
Ephesians it says:

Slaves, be obedient to those who are your earthly masters,
with fear and trembling, in singleness of heart, as to

Christ; not in the way of eye-service, as men-pleasers, but as servants of Christ, doing the will of God from the heart. (Eph: 6:5–6)

You will be serving Christ Himself if you approach your daily tasks in this way.

Our daily life has its share of trials and suffering; is a cross in many ways. Embrace the cross, give yourself to it, and it will become your joy and the door to transfiguration and deep union, the door that releases the power of God into your life; in weakness there is strength. Holding back from the cross makes it hurt more, makes the process of our purification even more painful; embracing it allows God to work quickly and do what He needs to do to move us on. Embrace being a mother, embrace taking care of the children with your whole heart; with your whole heart give yourself to it. Embrace being a lawyer and serving your clients as Christ Himself, for Christ does come to you in them. Embrace being a factory worker, as faithful service to Christ Himself, and it will be. Let go. Don't hold on to your own life. Die, and discover yourself alive. Let go of caring for yourself and your own interests, and discover how Christ is caring for you.

In the relationship between a husband and wife one of the things that dams up the love of a husband and his care for his wife, is her insisting on caring for herself, not allowing him to do it, perhaps because she doesn't trust him. The same is true in the relationship of a person to Christ. If we try to be our own head and take care of ourself and our own interests, we choose to live in a basic insecurity, knowing how fragile and vulnerable our own resources are. If we choose to let Christ be our head and care for us, it frees Him to do so. Let Christ care for you and see to your interests, and you embrace the cross of your daily life with your whole heart; and discover Him in it.

Accept the grace and the opportunity He's giving you for five minutes of quiet for prayer while nursing the baby, or at the end of your lunch break, and respond to that and you'll be given more. Grumble and complain about it, and you pull back from where God is for you now, and where He's willing to meet you now, where He knows you need to be met. Enter through the door He provides, not through the door you prefer. One leads to life; the other leads nowhere. Even though it may lead to life for another man, it won't for you. Relate on God's terms not your terms. Let Him care for your life. He will.

Gerard Manley Hopkins wrote a poem called *The Windhover* and I'd like to share a line with you as it expresses so well what we're talking about regarding daily faithfulness in small things, and the effects that this way of living produces. "Sheer plod makes plough down sillion shine and blue bleak embers, . . . fall, gall themselves and gash gold vermillion." In the dust and routine of our daily life, as we are faithful to Him in small things, to the extent that we are, He moves us along quickly to Himself. It seems slow from day to day, but in fact it is like being on a speeding train hurtling through a dark night. We are being brought quickly to Him. Our life is passing rapidly. The forms of this life are passing away, and only the eternal will remain, only that which is in Christ, joined and united with Him. God broods over us with a mighty love; God calls with a deep love and has imprinted that call in the primordial reaches of our being; our hearts are restless and they won't rest until they rest in Him. Hear the call, it's getting louder, but don't lift your head yet from your hoe, from your pencil, from tying your child's shoe; allow Him to join your heart to His while tying the shoe. Allow Him to move you through space and time to eternity while still tying the shoe. Hear the call, it's getting louder, it's drawing us deeper.

Now we can lift our heads. He is coming. He is walking toward us across a field with a crowd of laughing children. He is smiling. We can run to Him, stumbling through our sorrow and tears and gladness and relief; we can run, stumbling to Him. Now. We are one.

Chapter 1

1. Outler, Dr. Albert, *New Covenant*, Vol. 1, September 1971, p. 17.

2. Suenens, Cardinal Leo Josef, *New Covenant*, Vol. 3, October 1973, p. 7.

3. See, for example, the following excerpt from a widely respected book written in the Catholic tradition of spirituality and prayer. It provides a remarkably intelligible and touching picture of the striving toward genuine life in the Spirit, characteristic of this tradition, revealing both its grandeur and its poverty. Italics are mine.

   No matter how many times we renew our good intention to turn our thoughts to God, the simple truth of the matter is that we fail frequently. *Voluntary acts are never more than acts* whereas prayer must become a state, a permanent activity . . . What artificial means were proposed to try to approach this ideal! . . . Such means can never lead us to the end and we are very conscious of this fact that they are so many expedients. To be sure, they are excellent; they must be used, but they are but a step toward something more profound. *To interrupt the flow of life every now and then and turn our thoughts to God* gives us but a fragmentary union. And no matter how frequent these returns are, they are but transitory and never achieve an enduring union. To bring about this kind of union, another element, something more intimate, more vital is required: love, an ardent, invading, dominating love that impregnates life, becomes life itself and transforms into itself all our activities . . . The problem therefore is to reach a degree of fervor where love plays this unifying role . . . The man whose heart has fallen in love with God never grows tired of prayer. He alone will reach the summit of the unitive way . . .

All that is lacking is the touch of the Spirit. This, in truth, is everything, but the soul for its part is ready. This prayer (of simple regard or quiet), by its very nature stimulates and enkindles love. Now, this ardent love is the domain of the Paraclete, his gift par excellence and the essence of the mystical life . . . The soul already receives some small fragments of this gift and they will make it eager for more . . . Without a shadow of a doubt, the more God acts during mental prayer the better that prayer is, the soul obeying the inspirations which God himself awakens in it. He is now beginning to make a light and a new love mysteriously break through, even if feebly, in a scarcely apparent way, and in simple cooperation with the action of the soul, so much so that the latter is now aware of this. In fact, it may have the impression that it is drawing all of this from itself and that there is nothing new about its manner of praying, except a more marked degree of intensity and depth. But the truth is that these are the effect of the action of God. Already there is a latent influx of Holy Spirit and of isolated mystical elements, still not very distinct and mixed with human activity. The mystical state has not yet been reached but rather a premystic state, the last evolution of active mental prayer which by the combined operation of man and God, is an immediate preparation for contemplative prayer.

There is, as we see, a continuity between the two kinds of prayer. Nevertheless they are essentially different. The definite preponderance of the gifts of the Holy Ghost which, in mystical prayer, shed on the soul lights and a love directly infused from on high make it definitely passive under the divine influence. This will have to be made more precise. *It is, in truth, a new phase of the prayer life which is about to begin, in which there will no longer be any question of an "art of prayer," but an overflow in the soul of a completely supernatural prayer in which the Spirit himself prays in us "with unutterable groanings" (Rom. 8:26). This prayer of contemplation presents such peculiar characteristics, the conduct to be assumed differs so radically from what it previously should have been, and the number of those who reach it is so few that it seemed best to make a separate study of contemplation . . . For the moment, all I can do is point out to the reader that already visible Promised Land and urge him to walk courageously down the road that leads to it. Contemplation is the term to which the life of prayer normally tends. That should encourage us. But only they cross the threshold of divine ravishments who have first learned and practiced the art of prayer with perseverance.*

From *The Art of Prayer*, Martial Lekeux, Franciscan Herald Press, 1959, pp. 251–252, 360.

4. *New Covenant*, Vol. 1, March 1972, p. 5.

5. Fr. Michael Scanlan, *New Covenant*, Vol. 1, June 1972, pp. 4–5.

6. Bishop Joseph McKinney, *New Covenant*, Vol. 1, September 1971, pp. 11–13.

7. Hallesby, O., *Prayer*, trans. Clarence J. Carlsen, (Minneapolis, Minnesota: Augsburg Publishing House, 1931, 1959), p. 38.

8. Ibid. p. 92.

9. Tozer, A. W., *The Pursuit of God* (Harrisburg, Pennsylvania: Christian Publication, Inc.), pp. 16–17.

10. Johnson, Robert, *The Church Society of College Work Report*, Vol. XXXI, No. 1, p. 3.

11. Van Dusen, H. quoted in *They Speak with other Tongues*, J. Sherrill (New York: Pyramid Books, 1965), p. 28, 29.

12. Simpson, Charles, *New Covenant*, Vol. II, August 1972, pp. 10–14.

Chapter 2

1. Lewis, C. S., *Mere Christianity* (New York: Macmillan Paperbacks, 1961), pp. 55–56.

Chapter 4

1. Von Trapp, Maria, *New Covenant*, Vol. I, October 1971, pp. 4–6.

2. Books such as *The Pentecostal Movement in The Catholic Church* by Edward O'Connor, *The Baptism in the Holy Spirit as an Ecumenical Problem* by Kilian McDonnell, O.S.B. and Arnold Bittlinger, and *Catholic Pentecostalism: Problems in Evaluation* by Kilian McDonnell contain bibliographic clues that can put the interested reader in touch with this ongoing theological reflection.

3. Different denominational charismatic offices:
Catholic Charismatic Renewal Services
Communication Center
Drawer A
Notre Dame, Indiana 46556

Lutheran Charismatic Renewal
Coordinating Committee
% Larry Christenson
1450 W. Seventh St.
San Pedro, California 90732

American Baptist Charismatic Fellowship
% Ken Pagard
First Baptist Church
494 E Street
Chula Vista, California 92010

Charismatic Communion of Presbyterian Ministers
428 N.W. 34th
Oklahoma City, Oklahoma 73118

Episcopal Charismatic Fellowship
100 Colorado Boulevard
Denver, Colorado 80206

4. McDonnell, Kilian, O.S.B. From a private conversation.

5. Tugwell, Simon, *Did You Receive the Spirit?* (New York: Paulist Press/Deus Books, 1972), pp. 52–55.

6. Ibid., p. 69.

7. Prayer group directories are available from the Communication Center, Drawer A, Notre Dame, Indiana 46556. These are predominantly Catholic charismatic groups; other denominational groups will be putting out directories in the future. Many of these groups provide Life in the Spirit Seminars, which provide a simple but ordered way for interested Christians to approach a deeper life in the Spirit.

Chapter 5

1. Martin, Francis, *New Covenant*, Vol. II, July 1972, pp. 14–15.

2. A catalogue of books and tapes, many of which are suitable for spirtual reading and listening, is available by writing the Communication Center (see ftn. 7, Chapter 4). Also of interest is *New Covenant*, the monthly magazine that has developed from the Catholic charismatic renewal. Ecumenical in perspective, it is published at P. O. Box 102, Ann Arbor, Michigan 48107.

3. Ensley, Eddy, an unpublished manuscript to appear in *New Covenant*:

Numbers of music historians, in their attempts to understand the roots of Western music, have researched the common practice of congregations and individual Christians of this period using wordless singing as a means of praising God. Most of the Church Fathers laud this practice. Jubilation (L. jubili—shouts or sounds of joy), "wordless praise," "wordless psalms," and the "singing of alleluia," were some of the terms used to describe this singing of wordless hymns. Augustine, perhaps, defines it best. He states that Jubilation is a breaking forth into a singing of a vowel sounds. He furthermore states: "What is jubilation? Joy that cannot be expressed in words; yet the voice expresses what is conceived within and cannot be explained in words: this is jubilation . . . He who sings a jubilus does not utter words: he pronounces a wordless sound of joy; the voice of his soul pours forth happiness as intensely as possible, expressing what he feels without reflecting on any particular meaning. To manifest his joy the man does not use words that can be pronounced and understood, but he simply lets his joy burst forth without words; his voice then appears to express a happiness so intense that he cannot formulate it." (Emar. in Ps. 94, 3; 99, 4.)

The attitude of the Church Fathers toward jubilation is well summarized by the music historian Albert Seay who said of this wordless song: "It was an overpowering expression of the ecstasy of the Spirit, a joy that could not be restricted to words . . . It occupied a peculiar place in the liturgy, for it carried implications of catharsis, a cleansing of the soul." (Albert Seay, *Music in the Medieval World*).

The pioneer of biblical studies, St. Jerome, said: "By the term jubilus we understand that which neither in words nor syllables nor letters nor speech is it possible to express or comprehend how much man ought to praise God." (*Commentary on Ephesians:* P.L. XXVI, 970). St. John Chrysostom, contemporary of Jerome and Augustine, and the silver-tongued bishop of Constantinople said: "It is allowed to sing psalms without words, as long as the mind resounds within. For, we do not sing for men, but for God, who can hear even our hearts and penetrate into the secrets of our soul." (Eiston Psalmon XLI, in PGL, LV, col. 156.)

This singing of wordless hymns was widespread during this period. Marie Pieriki in her book *The Song of the Church* said: "This ejaculation modulated on all forms, became the refrain of gladness which accompanied the daily occupations of the peaceful population converted to the new faith."

Jubilation, in a free, improvised Spirit-led form appears to have been a major part of the life of the Christian Church at least till the first part of the seventh century. Cassiodorus, writing in the late sixth century, describes how a congregation sang wordless praise: "The tongue of the singers rejoices in it; joyfully the community repeats it; . . . (it is) an ornament for the tongue of singers . . . (it is) like an inexhaustible treasure, it is renewed in ever varying melodies."

The wordless singing of the Christians, while paralleled by qualitatively different secular equivalents, was, as the Jewish music scholar Alfred Sendrey points out, "born with the new religion" (Alfred Sendrey, *Music in Ancient Israel*, p. 202).

While the flowing melismatic aspect of the Gregorian chant developed from this free-style jubilation, the jubilation of this period was more expressive of joyful ecstasy and improvised. The first manuscripts of Gregorian chant are hundreds of years later and far different from the freer jubilation of the Fathers.

Chapter 6

1. The May 1974 issue of *New Covenant* was devoted to an explanation of "inner healing."

Chapter 7

1. U.S., Canadian and international prayer group directories are available from the Communication Center (see ftn. 7, Chapter 4).

Chapter 9

1. The text of the Pope's remarks is as follows:

And now a word to the members of the Grottaferrata congress.

We rejoice with you, dear friends, at the renewal of spiritual life manifested in the Church today, in different forms and in various environments. Certain common notes appear in this renewal: the taste for deep prayer, personal and in groups, a return to contemplation and an emphasizing of praise of God, the desire to devote oneself completely to Christ, a great availability for the calls of the Holy Spirit, more assiduous reading of the Scripture, generous brotherly devotion, the will to make a contribution to the service of the Church. In all that, we can recognize the mysterious and discreet work of the Spirit, who is the soul of the Church.

Spiritual life consists above all in the exercise of the virtues of faith, hope and charity. It finds its foundation in the profession of faith. The latter has been entrusted to the pastors of the Church to keep it intact and help it to develop in all the activities of the Christian community. The spiritual lives of the faithful, therefore, come under the active pastoral responsibility of each bishop in his own diocese. It is particularly opportune to recall this in the presence of these ferments of renewal which arouse so many hopes.

Even in the best experiences of renewal, moreover, weeds may be found among the good seed. So a work of discernment is indispensable; it devolves upon those who are in charge of the Church, "to those to whose special competence it belongs, not indeed to extinguish the Spirit, but to test all things and hold fast to that which is good." (cf. 1 Th. 5:12, 19–21; *Lumen Gentium*, 12.) In this way the common good of the Church, to which the gifts of the Spirit are ordained (cf. 1 Cor. 12:7), makes progress.

L'Osservatore Romano, October 11, 1973.